CHINA, EUROPE AND THE ANGLO-SPHERE

A COMPARATIVE ANALYSIS

China, Japan, Europe and the Anglo-Sphere
A Comparative Analysis

ALAN MACFARLANE

CAM RIVERS
PUBLISHING

2018

First published in Great Britain in 2018 by
Cam Rivers Publishing Ltd
5 Canterbury Close
Cambridge CB4 3QQ

www.cambridgerivers.com
press@cambridgerivers.com

Author: Alan Macfarlane

Copyright © Alan Macfarlane, 2018

Editor: Sarah Harrison
Marketing Manager: James O'Sullivan
Typesetting and cover design: Jaimie Norman

ISBN 978-1-912603-26-8

To the memory of

John Davey (1945 - 2017)

Friend, editor, publisher

Contents

Preface: why I wrote the book

THIS BOOK IS a continuation of the Wang Gouwei lectures (2011) and the subsequent book, *The Invention of the Modern World*. Like the lectures and book, it is mainly written for a Chinese audience. In the earlier book, I tried to explain modernity in its English form through my own experience but the need for such a book of cross-cultural explanation appears to be even greater half a decade later. China as it rapidly expands through the 'One Belt and One Road' initiative, is becoming ever more involved with other civilisations and needs to understand them. So this book is both a continuation of the previous task, but on a magnified scale since I am trying to move beyond the Anglosphere to include two other civilisations, Japan and Europe.

The book, a sequel to my book on Japan, is based on a combination of reading, experience through travel and sustained observation in the countries in question and conversations with people from the different civilisations. 'Japan' was finally written, after some eight visits over a period of fifteen years, and deep conversations with only half a dozen individuals.

This volume is based on sixteen visits to China, and a number to Europe as well as long immersion in Britain. The Chinese encounter is also longer in time, some 21 years since we first visited in 1996. Also, the conversations with Chinese from many backgrounds on our expeditions, as well as a number of research students and close friendships, are much more extensive. Furthermore, there is an added dimension with the Chinese encounter in that I have been engaged in numerous projects - workshops, summer schools, visiting Professorships, lecture tours, exhibitions, conferences, festivals, publishing and other joint projects – with Chinese partners. This has given me an insight into the inner dynamic of Chinese society in a way which one cannot gain just as a traveller or reader. I have been able to test out my guesses on a number of very intelligent younger Chinese, who are thanked in the acknowledgements.

I write this book now for a number of reasons which suggest that it may be particularly timely. Firstly there is the obvious and huge growth of China - phenomenal changes even in the years we have been visiting, and with the potential for massive growth in the future. People outside China need to understand China, which is and will influence their lives in the years ahead.

Secondly there is the often ill-informed and outmoded attitude of many outside China. Most people outside China know almost nothing about its history and culture, and a combination of an often-biased journalism and mounting fear at its success, distorts what little they do know. Even those in neighbouring countries, particularly Japan, often have a very distorted knowledge of Chinese history and Chinese people. Currently, the confrontations are being ramped up by a belligerent American stance which could lead to disaster.

In terms of my own life's trajectory and writing, this book is a knitting together of all experience and reading, starting from England, then through Nepal and North-East India to Japan and finally to China. My books started as small and localized studies such as 'Witchcraft', 'Ralph Josselin', 'Resources and Population', 'Individualism' in the 1970's, and then moving up to a more global level a level with political philosophy from Montesquieu to Fukuzawa in 'Riddle' and 'Making' and in-depth comparison between England and Japan in 'Savage Wars' in the 1990's. Now, after general surveys written between 2000 and 2005 in 'Glass', 'Tea' and 'Letters to Lily', I want to draw on all of this work and then to set it into another, civilisational, context.

This is very much a first approximation. The subject, four great and ancient world civilisations, is so large and complex that any one person can only grasp part of it. This is not a strictly academic book in the sense that it is not filled with footnotes and is not written in a complex style. Many assertions may seem bald and perhaps over-confident. They are based on the idea that after a lifetime of studies, one should make the results as clear and simple as possible.

My mentor in this is Tocqueville and it is worth quoting a little of his defence of the fact that his last great work, *L'Ancien Regime*, appeared to be very simple, but was the tip of an iceberg. Tocqueville worked for eight years in the archives of European civilisation and thought deeply. In the preface to the work he wrote:

> *I can say, I think, without too much boasting, that the book, which I now publish, is the product of very great labour. Quite a short chapter has sometimes cost me more than one year's research. I could have packed with notes the bottom of my pages; I have preferred only to insert a few notes and to place then at the end of the volume with a reference to the pages of the text to which they refer. In the notes will be found illustrations and proofs. I could supply many others, if anyone thinks it worth the while to ask for them.'*

I have relied very heavily on visits and conversations in the various civilisations I described. Each new visit shows me new facets and undiscovered corners, makes me understand things in a new way. Hence the work is always in progress. As C. Wright Mills put it, every book is provisional. One accumulates knowledge, and then sorts it out by working on it. He describes '...that the idea and the plan came out of my files, for all projects with me begin and end with them, and books are simply organized release from the continuous work that goes into them.

I am aware of the danger of 'essentialisation'. My approach, which is to look for the 'spirit of the laws', the 'deep grammar' of a civilisation, in the tradition of Montesquieu, Tocqueville,

Fukuzawa and others, is currently unfashionable. Perhaps because everything seems to be in such flux, many feel that culture is more contingent, accidental, creative and changing. Many do not like a stress on continuities, on permanent differences, on essential features – at best it is regarded as a conservative approach, stressing the need for preservation, at the worst it can lapse into apparent racism and determinism.

Nevertheless, I persist in my approach because I believe in the continuities and I also believe that given the vast amount of information that the history of the world presents, some simplifying techniques are essential. The path of caution would have been to qualify many of my ideas, to use the words 'probably' 'perhaps', 'but not in the south', 'sometimes', and other qualifiers. This would have perhaps made the account less contentious, but also, I have always thought, less useful. As one of teachers (and friends) Hugh Trevor-Roper once put it, 'One fruitful error is worth a thousand stale truths'. I have tried to avoid errors, but even the errors may sometimes (note the qualification) be useful.

Finally, I should point out that it may appear that the treatment of China is confined mainly to the first chapter. In fact, this is just a preliminary overview. It is only when we start to move away from China, to compare it to Japan which is so alike and so different, and then to the monotheisms of Europe and the Anglo-Sphere, that we really begin to understand what is special about China, and what is special about each of these civilisations in turn. Especially in the comparative chapters in the second half, I move beyond taking each civilisation in isolation and try to see what is in common, and what is different as a set of four great experiments in how millions of people can live through time.

Understanding Civilisations

MOST OF US tend to live in the present. This means that we are buffeted by recent events and by the sensational headlines they evoke. It seems as if the world, as my daughter would say, is 'quite a scary place'. Many old certainties and securities are crumbling. We are constantly being told that we are living in a new global world, with unprecedented challenges and changes. This is partly true. What is occurring now is a change in the speed and depth of what has happened for many millennia. Standing back from the present and putting it into perspective, it is easy to single out several converging pressures which lead to our confusion and anxiety.

One dramatic change is the ever-more rapid movements of large numbers of peoples, usually from poorer countries to what are perceived to be richer ones. The flow from Africa and the Middle East into Europe is a prime example. Another is the growing tide of desperate people moving from Central and Southern America towards the north. This suddenly lands people with neighbours whose culture and customs they know little about. Many feel threatened and sometimes angry.

We have coped with a world where thousands are on the move, now it is millions and the mixture of horror and sorrow we feel as we watch them scrabbling and sometimes drowning is, in my memory, unprecedented. Of course, there have been events like this before, for example at the partition of India, or at the end of the Second World War in Europe, but at that time people did not see the tragedies daily on screens in their houses.

Numerous sub-communities of people with very different

cultures and histories are being formed in almost every part of the world. Trying to understand how to handle this, how much conformity and how much tolerance there should be, how far the new influx threatens supposedly 'core' identities in the host nations, is one of the largest problems of our time.

The anxiety and confusion is increased by the constant bombardment of alternative cultural styles and models of life through modern communications technology. This increases the speed, diversity and volume of the pressures. We not only have food and material objects from all over the world, but challenges to our deeper cultural customs. When I was at University in Oxford in the 1960's, the major flow of ideas was between Europe and America. Now we live in a turbulent, multi-polar, world with ripples spreading out rapidly from all over the world.

Even with the developments of the second half of the twentieth century, ideas and fashions moved more slowly, through films, television, telephones and the movement of individuals. The era of the Internet, email, social media, smart phones and 24-hour reporting, means that things move in a flash, whether in the markets, fashion or politics. It is a confusing and never ceasing surge of information which has integrated even the remotest communities.

The rapidity of information flow due to the developments in computers and the internet is only a part of the consequences of something which is de-stabilizing all our lives, but of which we tend not to be consciously aware. The fact that the world is changing faster and faster occurs as a result of the law that states that technological growth in a world of applied science tends to be exponential. We are very much entwined with our material environment, for technology is rightly defined as 'the extensions of man'.

These pressures are related to another, which is the rapid

shift of power at the global level. We can see that up to two hundred and fifty years ago the largest, richest and most powerful nations on earth were in Asia, particularly China and India. Then, for the next quarter of a millenium, the pendulum swung to the West, reaching its highest point in the middle of the twentieth century. Then it has started to swing back towards the East.

Asia is already on an economic level with the West, with the Chinese economy by some reckonings the largest in the world and it is likely soon to overtake the United States in real terms. As Samuel Huntington put it, 'by the middle of the twenty-first century, if not before, the distribution of economic and manufacturing output among the leading civilisations is likely to resemble that of 1800. The two-hundred-year Western "blip" on the world economy will be over.'

The effects will be enormous, not just the rise of yet another great power but an unprecedented and never-to-be-repeated shift of another order. Many believe that the twenty-first century will be the era when Asia, and particularly China, becomes the dominant part of the world. We can already see the effects of this in our economies and cultures, but very few people in the West know much about Chinese, Japanese or other Asian cultures, or how they differ from that of the West.

In reverse, China and other Asian civilisations are grappling with the problem of how to absorb what is best in western technologies, social structures, legal systems, educational methods and politics without losing their own identities and historical traditions. This has been a problem for well over a century in Japan and India, and it is a huge problem for China as it emerges as one of the economic and political superpowers. Many Chinese know little about the deeper structure of Western cultures. A simple explanation may help them to choose what to accept and what to reject.

A final major cause of anxiety is international political anarchy, the dissolution of any sort of agreed framework for world politics in our shrunken globe. As we watch the collapse of much of the belt from North Africa to Afghanistan, which apparently no one can do much about, as well as dangerous confrontations on the borders of Russia, we feel that we are at another time of the dissolution of the old rules.

The new communications technologies, plus the shifts of the balance of power, reminds us is that we live now in an interconnected world, where the coexistence of enduring and powerful blocks, that is civilisations, is going to be with us for decades and probably centuries. There is no point in trying to force these civilisations into becoming one – a uniform, or global, world civilisation. We have to live with this tenacious set of blocks that have been created by the tides of world history. This makes mutual understanding between civilisations absolutely essential. How can this be achieved through a radical rethink of our world and our attitudes? We can make a start by defining civilisations and working out a simple method of reducing their complexity to a level where we can understand and compare them.

Understanding civilisations

A civilisation is not an empire because it is not always held together by one central power. Yet people within it are linked by a shared language, ideology (sometimes of a religious kind), and various customs and cultural features. It makes those who inhabit the civilisation feel, in opposition to other civilisations, the sense of 'We'. We the Chinese, Japanese, Europeans or inhabitants of the 'Anglosphere'.

Style, culture and identity now spread across the political divisions of states with the ever richer types of communications technologies, so there are grounds for thinking that civilisations are the main unit which dominate the planet. If this is correct, then in trying to think about the future peace of the world we should concentrate our attention on them.

It has been suggested that there is a deep set of structuring dispositions which shape our lives. This is a mixture of unexamined ideas, bodily practices, ways of feeling which shape us in our childhood. These dispositions are normally invisible, just leaving their trace on the surface in formal religious, economic, political, legal, social, intellectual and other systems. These 'habits of the heart' and mind lie behind the everyday surface of life. If we can make the rules more explicit we will start to understand our world better.

One of the most successful attempts to understand civilisations is to be found in the work of the French thinker Alexis de Tocqueville. In his books on *Democracy in America* (1835, 1840) and *L'Ancien Regime* (1856), we find deep insights into three civilisations – France, England and America. Each civilisation is distinct and different, yet he makes it possible to understand all three. Tocqueville shows how 'the point of origin' as he calls it, that is the deep history of each, has shaped it and led to those structural relations which determine the past and future. Yet how did he achieve this?

One of his methods is a broadly comparative approach. Throughout his writings he was holding three or four civilisations in his mind (for he was also interested in North Africa and India). Through constant contrasts and comparisons, explicit and often implicit, each case is illuminated. These comparisons made his own culture of France strange and clear before him. They also made it possible for him to enter a new world in America.

Second, Tocqueville sought to understand the world by shifting the gaze from particular things, for example music, politics, the family, to the *relation* between things, for example how politics and religion, or the family and economy, were related. It is in the balance and tension between elements in a culture that we will discover its deeper meaning. This can also be described as the 'holistic' approach, that is the consideration of a whole civilisation, rather than concentrating on one part of it.

The third feature was Tocqueville's combination of history and anthropology. Having lived through the French Revolution and being part of an ancient family, Tocqueville realised the importance of history. He knew that we can only understand a civilisation if we go back through the centuries. An approach which is merely based on the present is bound to be shallow. On the other hand, he also realised that a historical approach, without a real analysis of the present, is equally unsatisfactory. It will lack a grasp of what the real questions are. So history without anthropology is narrow, while anthropology without history is shallow.

To describe a civilisation requires more than hard thinking. It requires empathy, intuition and personal involvement. This is why very few have succeeded in providing a convincing account of a world civilization. An account of some of the difficulties we face when trying to understand civilizations was written by one of the greatest of anthropologists, A. L. Kroeber. Kroeber points out that such portraits stand on the boundary between art and science. He also insists that the principal thing that is needed is empathy, and a willingness to suspend our own ethnocentric value judgements.

Yet even with the tools of comparison, origins, intuition, the task is immense. It is bound to lead to oversimplification and distortion. It will reveal ignorance across such a wide spectrum. Yet I believe that even if it is partially successful it may be worth the attempt.

Among other things it may help readers to understand the unfamiliar that is assailing them every day. Constantly presented with rapid and unfamiliar cultural models, it is tempting to withdraw into a narrow isolationism. Since we live in a highly volatile, militarized and in many ways aggressive world, a little more understanding might help to avert some of the tragedies which unfold before us.

Furthermore, by giving different mirrors it may make it easier to understand ourselves. We each live in a world which is so familiar and unexamined that it is usually impossible to stand back and understand why we are as we are or why we think as we do. In the words ascribed to Confucius, it is not going to be a fish that discovers water or a bird that discovers the air. Only when we leave our own secure world will we become aware of what so intimately surrounds us.

By definition, other civilisations are based on different premises to our own; their categories and logic are different. To enter into that alien world is extremely difficult, for it requires an imaginative leap, a suspension of disbelief and a temporary acceptance that our own world may not have all the answers.

How do we locate a civilisation? If it is a cultural style, identity, way of life, it tends not to be coterminous with physical borders. It is not like a state or nation, but much wider, a cultural system that can be found far from its original homeland. Thus Chinese, Islamic or European civilisation is not confined to China, the Middle East or America. A big city may contain many civilisations.

For this reason I prefer to use a looser term to describe civilisations, namely 'sphere'. Sphere means something like 'sphere of influence' or 'sphere of culture'. I will append the word 'sphere' to the main noun. I first encountered this usage in the work of James Bennett in his seminal book, *The Anglo-sphere Challenge* (2004), where he describes something much wider than England, or even England and America, but rather the whole wide swathe of the English-speaking and influenced world. Thus, I will tend not to write of Chinese civilisation, but of the Sinosphere. Spheres ripple outwards and can co-exist, piled up on one another and inter-acting in complex ways.

There is also the choice of which civilisations or spheres I should include. My book began in part as a reply to Samuel P. Huntington's *The Clash of Civilisations* (1997), and this helped me to start isolating major civilisations. He classified the world into nine civilisations in all. I have modified his scheme considerably and reduced the number I shall deal with from nine to four. I have selected what I consider to be distinct spheres, and ones which I know personally through ravelling, reading, teaching and friendships.

Four
Civilisations

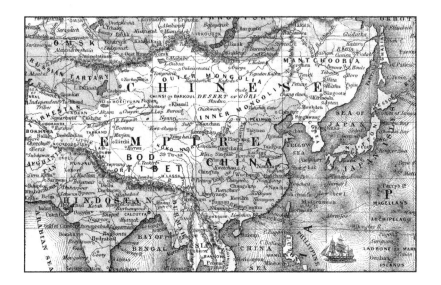

The Sinosphere

CHINA CONTAINS OVER a fifth of humankind. It has arguably the longest continuous civilisational history on earth, stretching back at least five thousand years. Many of the important technologies in the world were developed first in China and were then transferred to the West. These included the three which the philosopher Francis Bacon singled out as the basis of the modern world; the magnetic compass, the printing press and gunpowder.

For almost all of the last three thousand years China has been the most powerful, wealthy and inventive civilisation on earth. It continued so until about 1820. Then, for a brief two hundred years, a mere breath in its great history, it was mauled by predators from outside, first Britain and the West, then Japan. Now it is re-emerging from a century and a half of turmoil inaugurated by the First Opium War of 1839-42 and ending with the liberalization of China with Deng Xiaoping from 1979.

It seems likely that China will again become the largest economy on earth within a generation. It currently represents the second-biggest economy in the world behind the U.S. and is projected to grow by 5.8% this year. It has more than double the GDP of Japan which ranks third in terms of GDP, and over half that of the U.S. or Europe. Its economy is doubling every eight to ten years. In terms of the amount which people can purchase, given the value of the currency and costs (purchasing power parity), China is already the largest economy in the world. Yet *what*, exactly, is happening and *why* are almost unknown to outsiders. But we need to know, for all of our present is already deeply affected by the fate of China. Our future will be even more so.

First impressions of China

For many westerners, the perception of China is conditioned by an often negative and suspicious press. So it is easy to obtain a negative image of China. The western media usually accepts that China has had considerable material growth, and even concedes that this is largely what has contributed to a fall in the number of the absolutely poor on earth in the last two decades, lifting over 700 million people above the poverty line, while the rest of the world only lifted a quarter of this at the most. Yet admiration for this extraordinary achievement is very quickly qualified with warnings that China has destroyed as much as it has created.

So when I first went to China in 1996, here is what I had in the back of my mind from small snippets of information which were filtering out through television and newspapers.

Here is how I summarized my views on China before I went there.

We are warned of the vast ecological destruction, symbolized by the largest dam in the world at the bottom of the Three Gorges on the Yangtze, which is covering much of archaeological value and displacing millions of people. We are told of growing inequalities. The rich become rapidly richer, even if the poor also slightly improve their position. So the gaps, particularly between the more affluent city dwellers and rural peasants grow dangerously large. Everywhere the old communal values induced by communism are being undermined by a crass materialism and individualism.

Sweated labour was always a characteristic of the energy-scarce and industrious Chinese way of life. Now, we are told, the conditions in China's industrial revolution are similar to the appalling sweat-shops of nineteenth century Liverpool or Manchester. Crowds of unprotected immigrants are flooding into the cities. Paid miserably, often injured by machinery, living in virtual slave dormitories, it is they who lie behind the Chinese miracle which has made 'Made in China' the stamp of our world.

Finally, we are often given a picture of political and religious persecution. We are told that the Chinese authorities persecute religious minorities like the Falun Gong today, as they persecuted Christian missionaries in the nineteenth century. Political dissenters are kept in detention centres and labour camps without trial. The days of the worst excesses may be over, but we are warned that we can see the underlying attitude of the Chinese government in the way it bulldozed and shot its own 'democracy' students in Tiananmen Square in 1989. Individual human rights, we are told, are absent. Ethnic minorities and in particular the Tibetans are oppressed. The press and the television are heavily censored.

As a western consumer of the 'free press', I accepted many of these negative stereotypes in the 1970's and 1980's; yet, when we visited China in 1996 we immediately found that most were either completely wrong, or hugely distorted. We went back in 2002 and found even less of the early picture was right. Since then we have been back fifteen times for a month or six weeks, and travelled round most parts of China except the far north west. We have travelled with my young Chinese students and visited many cities, towns and remote villages. We talked to many people from ordinary villagers to University Professors and government officials. I have worked with a number of Chinese Ph.D. students and given numerous lectures all across China. We have filmed several hundred hours of video and taken many photos – only in one village, on our first visit in 2002, were we asked not to film on our own.

Here is a simple overview of how I see China now, in 2018. No doubt my views will alter over the coming years, but this is an attempt to grasp the deeper structure of this vast civilisation.

The unity of written language

Because of its size and ancient roots, almost anything we say about China can be qualified. China as a unified State is well over two thousand years old. It stretches from areas similar to Scandinavia or Russia down to the southern Mediterranean. Furthermore, it is changing rapidly. Is there anything that can be said that is true of all this huge and varied country?

I believe there are some universal features, and it is because they are there that this extraordinary Empire was held together over such a long period. One great unifying bond is the written language, which has changed little for several thousand years.

To a Westerner, used to alphabetical scripts where a character represents a sound which, in combination, forms a word, it is difficult to understand the system of pictorial representations. Each character in Chinese is a word or 'logos', hence it is known as a logographic language.

The power and longevity of the writing system has kept China together, and lies behind its second great feature, literacy. If most societies are held together by the political system, the economy, the family, or by religion, China is the only civilisation I know of which is held together by an examination system. To understand how this began, we need to set it in a much wider context of power and administration.

The bureaucratic Empire

As I studied the later development of this extraordinary integrated civilisation I was mystified as to how and when it had begun. I knew that there were great civilisations for at least three or four thousand years before the Qin Emperor, spreading out from the Yellow River, and culminating in the period of the Warring States from about 475 B.C. to the victory of the Qin in 221 B.C.

This was when Confucius, Mencius and Laotze flourished and laid out their philosophies, but in the context of those warring times their ideas were only marginal. They were encased within a form of political organization which we can term 'feudal' and in that sense similar to that found in mediaeval Japan or the mediaeval West.

In this system, the rulers held their states together by delegating power to noble families, each with their own territories. They passed their family estates to their descendants from generation to generation. The Confucian meritocratic system had no real function here and it's peaceful philosophy of loyalty and harmony was irrelevant.

One of the states, the Qin, centred in western China, began to develop an entirely new system of government in the fourth century BC. This is largely associated with the ideas of the reforming figure of Shang Yang (390-338 BC). He was the Prime Minister of the Duke of Xiao, and one of the founders of what was later termed the Legalist philosophical system, though this is an inaccurate representation of a system based on much more than law and better described as 'methodological uniformity'.

Its implementation destroyed the feudal system of noble families and replaced it with a meritocratic bureaucracy. Henceforth, the top positions in the state were open to all, based on merit rather than blood. This also minimized the role of landowners so that China became a State where there were small and medium peasants and no dominating gentry class.

The effects of this huge change were combined with other profound reforms in taxation, administration and military efficiency (the use of recently developed weaponry, cavalry and better transportation) so that the economic and military power of the Qin kingdom grew. The outcome was that in 221 B.C. the Qin were sufficiently powerful to defeat the other states and the first Emperor of China, as he proclaimed himself, Emperor Chin Shi Huang, unified the Warring States.

In the fifteen years of his reign he set the template for the China we know to this day. He split the country into thirty-six administrative provinces, installed a standardized writing system that would cover the whole Empire (later known as Mandarin and based on the pictographic writing system). He unified the weights, measures and currency. He built many roads and bridges. He enforced Shang Yang's view that no individual in the state, however powerful, should be above the law. He endorsed the Legalist view that the only important people in the state were the top officials and the peasants. Those engaged in other professions, particularly merchants and traders, were inferior and regarded with suspicion – a trait which helps to explain the absence of an effective middle class throughout Chinese history. The suspicion of any power that threatened the ruler was later extended to religious organizations and helps to explain the weakness of Buddhism and other religions in China.

This was the context in which Confucius' vision of a system based on personal relations and on a meritocratic government recruited through written examinations could at last make sense. So China became the first great bureaucratic civilisation, held together by writing, law, officialdom and education, but with basically only two important groups, the civil service and the peasant-warriors.

The Emperor's vision was immense. The First Emperor saw China as an entity around which he started to build the Great Wall of China to keep the barbarians out and the Middle Kingdom intact. So China was now a bounded space. China was also bounded in time, for the Empire was founded in a notional Year Zero. The Emperor decreed that all books were to be burnt and anyone who hid a book was branded and made a slave for life.

In some ways the First Emperor's later emulator was Chairman Mao who tried to set up another type of wall, of a virtual kind, around China. He also tried to abolish history and the past with the Cultural Revolution. In these two cases we can see that only in a vast upheaval could an Empire as huge and diverse as China be changed permanently. Even they failed, for though much was changed, much also has survived both of their revolutions.

This first unification only lasted two years, with the death of the Qin Emperor, but the model survived so that within a few years of his death, China was unified again under the great Han state (which gave its name to the Chinese people) which was then to last for over four hundred years.

Under the Han, the Qin revolution was magnified but mellowed as the extreme and ruthless Legalistic philosophy fell out of favour and the message of Confucius and Laotze gained ascendancy. Yet the transformation to an unprecedented new kind of political and intellectual world had been achieved and it is the blueprint which helps us understand China today.

Since the Qin and Han, education, that is the passing on between the generations of basic skills in reading and writing, set within the transmission of ethical codes, has been the heart of Chinese civilisation. The education in itself is different from what has come to be considered 'education' in the West. It was based on learning the classics by heart, absorbing the ethical systems of Confucianism, learning the arts of bureaucratic government – loyalty, memory, discrimination, judgment and fairness. Family status and success in the examination system replaced an older aristocratic system.

So China became the only civilisation on earth which was held together by a largely meritocratic system where potentially anyone could reach the highest levels through mental ability. There was no longer any class of landed nobility, that main pillar of Japan and Indo-European systems.

At a stroke, the arts that were elevated were no longer hunting and fighting, but rather writing, painting, reading, music and thinking. It became the one civilisation which has put the mind and intellect at its core and unified millions of people over thousands of years by way of ideas of the true, the good and the beautiful. The written word became the symbol of unity and the scholar gentleman the highest calling.

When we look at China now we need to remember this 'point of origin', when one civilisation on Earth moved decisively to something entirely new in nature and scale – a bureaucratic, centralised, meritocratic, standardized and unified system able to hold together hundreds of millions of people century after century, whatever the shocks they were subjected to.

War and violence

This is a highly simplified story and should not be taken to mean that war and fighting have been unimportant in China. Up to the unification of China in 221 B.C., China was filled with warring armies and bloody wars. After the abolition of the landed aristocracy, the militarization may have decreased a little, but there were numerous later wars, including those of the Three Kingdoms (220-280 A.D.), involved huge armies. The Tang and then the Northern and Southern Song again saw a decline in internal warfare, but the threat from the Mongols made China a warlike place. Yet after the Mongol invasion, the clans and warriors were again weakened during the Ming dynasty.

The Manchu (Qing) dynasty from the middle of the seventeenth century was aggressive, expanding over a vast area to the west of China and incorporating it, and putting down minority rebellions, partly caused by its policy of taking over the administration of hitherto largely autonomous areas. Then in the nineteenth century China was subject to frequent attacks (including the Opium Wars) and vast civil wars, including the Taiping and Boxer rebellion. The twentieth century was one of terrible wars. For example, perhaps twenty million Chinese died as a result of the Sino-Japanese War from 1937 to 1945.

Yet, despite all this, one can say that while warfare was endemic, China was, compared to much smaller but highly divided Europe after the fall of Rome, relatively less riven by internal civil wars. There was no equivalent to the small states of Europe, with their later strong nationalism. Furthermore, while the Emperor had large numbers of armed troops, much of the defence of the country and local policing was done by peasant families who were settled in dangerous areas. In return for holding land they could be mobilized when there were invasions or civil disturbances.

It is all a matter of scale and degree. China, like all great civilisations, was originally founded on violence. Yet it is far from the extreme in this respect. Certainly in the period since the Second World War, if we compare China to the United States, the involvement in overseas wars is far less extreme in China. Although involved in Korea and Vietnam, there is nothing equivalent to the bombing of Vietnam, Cambodia and Laos, or the wars in Afghanistan, Iraq, or even the blockade of Cuba. 'Regime change' is an American, not a Chinese, speciality. The current expenditure of the United States on its military is much greater than that in China. America's spending in 2015 was 3% of its GDP, China's 1.2%. With $1821 per capita in America and $95 in China, so the total of American spending is nearly four times the amount of that in China.

One effect of all this is that the methods of war, the weapons and tactics, reached a high level, but did not develop as fast as they did in the warlike West. So that while the navies and armies of China were roughly on an equivalent level to those of western Europe in 1500, three centuries later the British could humble this mighty Empire in the two Opium Wars with far more advanced weaponry and training, with France, Germany, Russia and then Japan following.

Money and cities

One consequence of this elevation of the Confucian ideal was the downplaying, not only of war, but also of commerce and money. The Chinese have always been excellent businessmen and traders, highly interested in profit, money and marketing. They have had huge and busy cities and amazingly widespread and connected waterways. Yet the Confucian and Legalist ordering placed the making of money through trade and manufacture below the more honourable toil of peasants in the fields.

In China people were as eager to make money as anywhere and there were occasionally some large trading firms from the nineteenth century onwards (for example in Shanxi and the Yellow River delta). Yet the Mandarin attitude to money-making was somewhat dismissive. A combination of political uncertainties, the division of family wealth between all the children, and, later, foreign competition, meant that there was truth in the old Chinese saying that 'No rich (Chinese) family can remain rich for more than three generations'.

No large, independent estate or order, which is often termed the 'bourgeoisie', emerged until recently. It was difficult to pass on large economic gains to the next generation. Hence few huge family firms emerged, unlike in Japan, India or the West. The great cities had no independence in law and were just seats for the administration, so the town traders remained very vulnerable to government power.

The Confucian template

To someone familiar with the history of the small nation-states of the West, the whole Chinese structure is puzzling. How does a system, where a vast country was ruled by a few hundred thousand bureaucrats, without a large instituted police force or army or the support of an instituted middle-class and church, maintain order? And how has it managed to do so for most of two thousand years in what has often been a relatively peaceful and orderly Empire?

The secret seems to lie in another feature which is again simplest to explain in terms of Confucian thought. The heart of Confucian ethics was duty and responsibility between people. It is an ethical order based on the relationship of a pair of people, a dyadic or two-sided link which was replicated along the social and political dimensions.

The essence is the bond between parent and child, particularly the father and the son. This was the fundamental building block. The father's power was almost absolute. He could, in theory, do no wrong to his child and had power of life and death with no appeal. The child owed obedience and loyalty, the father protection and sustenance. The bond could not be broken or challenged. This relationship was then extended outwards in various ways.

One was in a generational direction. All those of a superior generation were owed duty and respect by the young. This obviously applied to the teacher, who was to be deeply revered and obeyed. It also applied between older and younger in the family – an older brother had power over a younger. It applied in relation to sex – women were by birth inferior and every woman owed respect and loyalty to all men.

In effect, this meant that the family became a total world. The child was part of the economic unit, run by the oldest close relative. He or she was part of a ritual unit, for only through the older relatives could the dead ancestors and other invisible powers be accessed. He or she was part of a political unit – the oldest relative stood for the Emperor. He or she was obviously part of a social unit, which arranged his or her education, marriage and contacts.

So China was largely self-administered within the millions of families, both the close family of grandparents, parents and children, but also more widely in the powerful clan system based on tracing one's ancestry through the male line. Such clans were self-governing ritual, economic, political and social units.

Crystallizing the wisdom of previous thinkers, Confucius had the genius to take this beyond kinship and to integrate it into the general political system by emphasizing the parallel between the relations of obedience and rule within the family and the governing of China. The Emperor was the father who held the system together. The way one behaved to one's father is the way one should behave to the Emperor. So, instead of having to delegate power to feudal, armed, nobles and give them landed estates as payment, the Emperor delegated power to the household heads and supported them if their children challenged them in any way.

When combined with a high esteem for the mass of the peasant producers, and the Confucian educational system which allowed a very bright son to move up to a position of wealth and power through education, this provided a universal lottery which gave all families hope and ambition. Furthermore, this system was policed by the very persons who performed well in the examination system and became the civil servants of the Emperor.

There were contradictions and tensions. The father's power was so great that the son could not approach him closely and did not necessarily feel any affection for him. Another tension was that, while the wife was in the power of her husband, she was also bound strongly to her family of origin and hence there was a concealed war between husband and wife. Another was that there was a potential conflict between loyalty to one's father and to the Emperor.

Another serious tension lay in the question of whether the Emperor could do wrong. Was he to be obeyed whatever he did? Here again there was a well-known resolution. The

Emperor's power came from the 'Mandate of Heaven' and that mandate could be withdrawn. Both a cause and a sign of such withdrawal were prolonged catastrophes, famines, wars, diseases which meant one could switch allegiances. Even his loyal followers, the Mandarin bureaucrats, had the duty to oppose the Emperor if they felt there was sufficient evidence to show he had lost the mandate.

Law and custom

The extraordinary integration of the system achieved through joining the power of the family and the bureaucracy had other effects. One was that it was unnecessary to have more than a minimal legal system, and that system has a number of significant differences from legal systems in the West.

The codes built on each other, but for simplicity let us take the Great Ming Code (Da Ming Lii), promulgated at the start of the Ming dynasty, that is about the middle of the fourteenth century. It had many overlaps with the earlier codes of the Tang from six hundred years earlier, and those of the Qing, four hundred years later.

Several things are particularly striking. One is that almost the whole code is concerned with criminal law, that is the relations between the State (Emperor) and his people. It is a penal law code. There is nothing on civil law, cases to be tried in imperial courts between imperial subjects.

If we compare the Ming code to the English work of Henry de Bracton *On the Laws and Customs of England*, a work written about a century before the Ming codes and more than ten times as long, it has an entirely different feel. Only a small part of Bracton is concerned with criminal law and punishments. The majority concerns the process of law, rights and duties, the way to deal with property and wealth.

By the middle of the eighteenth century when the Qing codes were not much more elaborate than the Ming, it took eight large volumes (over forty times the length of the Ming code) to cover English law in William Blackstone's *Commentaries on the Laws of England*. Ninety percent of this is concerned with civil law and the procedure of the courts.

Secondly, the Ming and other law codes, in their evaluation of the severity of crimes, are based on the social relationship of those involved – particularly family relationships. There are at the start of the Ming code elaborate tables of degrees of mourning relationship, based on patrilineal ties and marriage. Each offence is graded according to superiority and distance of relationship.

Thus, for example, to strike or kill a father or paternal grand-father, is far more serious than to kill or strike a brother or son or maternal grand-father. This embedded, status-based, law in China is completely different from the individualistic law in England where, in Bracton or Blackstone, family relationships are almost totally ignored. The Chinese code has strong resemblances to status-based continental Roman law.

A third feature is the absence of any guidance in the Ming code on due process. Whereas English law books are filled with regulations about how trials are to be held, what constitutes a legal charge, what is evidence, the rights and duties of judges, lawyers, plaintiffs and defendants, there is no hint of this in the Ming code.

It seems to be assumed that when a person was accused of a serious offence he or she will be summoned and questioned by a single magistrate, who would, if necessary, use torture and threats to arrive at some sort of truth. There is obviously no jury, no presumption of innocence, no idea of intrinsic legal rights. There is not even any mention or indication of lawyers in the courts, again a great difference.

Once found guilty, the punishments in the Ming code were ferocious. For example there are five degrees of beating with a light and heavy stick, five degrees of penal servitude, three degrees of life exile, and two degrees of death (strangulation and decapitation) and banishment. The penal servitude, for example, might involve being imprisoned in a heavy wooden 'cangue' (a wooden 'stocks' which imprisoned the head and hands) for months or years. There were other death penalties also, including 'death by slicing'.

The system appears to consist of a very simple set of punishments to maintain social order, to support the distinctions of family status, and the peace and order of this huge empire. An immensely complicated set of courts and procedures, paralleling those present in medieval to modern England to deal with contesting individuals and their rights and duties, especially in relation to property, as far as is now known, were less developed. We are in a world where people are born into a fixed and unequal position based on birth order, sex, parental status and relation to the Emperor. These status divisions are rigidly maintained by the imperial law codes.

Such a system remained in place over more than fifteen hundred years in China until less than two hundred years ago. Then reforms began to be made at the edges of the system. Yet it was only a hundred years ago with the fall of the Qing, that a new criminal code, based on that of Japan, was introduced. By this, collective responsibility of families in criminal matters was eliminated, corporal punishment and slavery abolished, and the use of torture forbidden. Some further progress had been made by the time of the Sino-Japanese war in 1937, but then for the next forty years, all serious movement towards a rights-based and 'modern' form of law was suspended.

Only after 1978, and with growing speed in only the last twenty years, has the whole legal system of China started to be changed to bring it into line with western practices. This is, in many ways, as large, and impressive an undertaking as the economic reforms, and indeed part of that whole procedure.

I have visited an intermediate level court in China and it now compares reasonably well in its process, care and rules with equivalent courts in the West. Discussing with various lawyers in China it is clear that a huge set of reforms have been introduced and, at least in theory, all litigants are treated as formally equal, and the 'rule of law', including the separation of law and politics, is being proclaimed. A large legal profession is being trained, with judges, barristers, lawyers and solicitors.

Yet the older system of avoiding taking cases to court still persists. Recently we visited a new 'model' village near Chengdu. In the administrative building there was a room labeled 'Police'. When we went in, we found only a large table and some chairs. We were told that if there was a dispute between neighbours or family, a policeman might be called. His aim was to bring in all those in the dispute and to try to get them to agree a solution to the differences through discussion, rather than taking the case to a higher court.

Social structure and the professions

The absence of a developed legal profession is only part of a wider absence of most of the professional groups we find in the West. We have seen that there was, over the last two thousand years, no warrior aristocracy, there were few professional lawyers, and hardly any large businessmen and industrialists. Other professional groups were also absent or weakly developed. For example, while there were teachers at the innumerable schools, and there were flourishing academies of a kind, the development of an independent third level university sector did not occur until the end of the nineteenth century. So there was no academic profession of the western kind.

Another numerous profession, the main pillar of education and literacy in the Indo-European and Anglosphere regions, the religious orders, were weak. There were from time to time monastic movements with the introduction of Buddhism, but these were hemmed in in the eighth to tenth centuries and never flourished independently again. The Taoists did not have full-time priests, although there were many hermits who retreated to remote woods and mountains to meditate. The Confucians produced scholars but not a priesthood.

Summarizing all this, China presents a powerful but simple profile. Unlike the fourfold structures of India, Japan and the West, China only had two tiers, the tiny ruling group, the civil servant and mandarins, and the huge majority of small workmen, merchants and the vast peasantry. There was only one ladder of preferment, through education up into the bureaucracy.

A structural civilisation

The essence of China lies in what has been called 'structuralism'. That is to say that the meaning of everything – human beings, nature, art, life – does not lie in *individual things* but in *relations*, and in the *relations of these relations*.

A popular representation of this is in the symbol of Yin and Yang, an independent pair, each necessary to the other while separate, while each containing a seed of the other. Sun and moon, earth and heaven, male and female, night and day, Emperor and subject, father and child, husband and wife, black and white, the binary oppositions are endless and in each case the single entity only has meaning *in its relation* to its paired contrast.

This does not just mean that A is linked to B, but we have A/B, where it is the relationship between, or structural tension between A and B that holds the system together. Each pairing also derives its meaning from being part of wider relations; man is to woman, as day is to night, as Emperor is to subject, as father is to child, and as heaven is to earth.

How the pairs relate to and reinforce each other accounts for the strength of Chinese civilisation and the durability of the relations. To challenge the father is to challenge everything, to challenge the male-to-female relation is to turn the world upside down. The whole is an interlinked system which joins together all the forces of power, wealth, society and belief into one single whole.

I had originally thought that this structural feature, so alien to western thought, was mainly the result of Confucianism, with its ethical system stressing the relationship between people, rather than the people themselves. Clearly this is part of the reason and in turn linked to the power of the Chinese family system where it is relationships to family which have, through thousands of years, made a person into an element of a group, not a single individual.

Recently, however I have found that the reasons for structuralism lie much deeper, stemming out of ancient philosophies which in turn became incorporated into Chinese Buddhism. This feature, technical though it is, needs to be grasped and it is worth explaining in a little more depth.

Peter Hershock, in an article on "Chan Buddhism" in 2017 explains this feature as follows.

Common to all Buddhist traditions are the teachings of interdependence and karma...
To help clarify the significance of this, Fazang made metaphorical use of a traditional, timber-framed building that is held together without any fasteners by the compressing force of gravity on all of its

parts (Huayan wujiao zhang, in Taishō shinshō daizūkyu, Vol. 45, no. 1866). Removing the clay roofing tiles and their immense weight would destabilize such a building, eventually causing it to collapse. But the roofing tiles are placed on top of purlins that are placed perpendicularly on rafters resting on a central ridge beam and on rim joists that are themselves resting on columns placed atop individual foundation stones. Since removing the roofing tiles of such a structure would cause the entire building to collapse, the tiles can be said to be the cause of the totality of the building. But the same is true for all of the other parts of the building. Similarly, each particular in the world (shi) consists at once in causing and being caused by the dynamic patterning (li) of the totality of all things. Each thing ultimately is what it means for all others.

❊❊❊

Such a way of looking at the world is so unfamiliar to western traditions, yet vital to understand. China has shown an extraordinary ability, unparalleled in world history, to expand to fill such a vast and diverse territory and to hold together many hundreds of millions of people.

All feel roughly equivalent, with the exception of some ethnic minorities, though even they are partially absorbed and tend to succumb in the end. The 'Han' model becomes the 'natural' model and, when joined and re-enforced by a logographic written language and spoken Mandarin in which all can communicate, the whole is one vast and joined 'chain of being'.

Such a chain is resilient. One thing that has always amazed me is the way in which, while always changing, China also remains the same. Many have noted this. For example, it has been observed that the law codes were much the same in the Han, Tang, Ming, Qing, lasting in essence at least two thousand years. The same is true of the basic philosophy. Confucius's precepts are as relevant and resonant today as they were two and a half thousand years ago. The same is true of fashions, of music, of painting, of dress, and of course of the ancient language, where an educated Chinese can still read texts written two thousand years ago.

If China had been a self-contained island, like Japan or England, able to absorb and reject invaders and free of massive civil wars, then it's unchanging nature might have been easier to understand. Yet it is a vast country with borders impossible to defend forever, especially from the powerful marauding nomads. So, in the last thousand years alone, it has been subject to four immense shocks which would have destroyed the foundations of any civilisation founded on a less simple, but tough, skeleton.

In the thirteenth century the Mongols conquered China, destroying many cities, killing perhaps a quarter or more of the population, ransacking and looting. Yet the Mongol dynasty, the Yuan, lasted for less than a hundred years. It absorbed, used and reformed a number of earlier Chinese administrative systems. Then in the seventeenth century another group of tribal invaders, the Manchus, again broke through and took over China. They were again absorbed, taking over the Mandate of Heaven and ruling through the Chinese bureaucracy. By using the existing structure, the Qing dynasty lasted for several centuries before collapsing.

It collapsed partly because of another shattering blow from the outside, this time from the West, in particular Britain in the mid nineteenth century Opium Wars. This weakened a China already beset by environmental problems, huge rebellions of which the Taiping and the Boxer uprisings were just the last. Yet though the Empire collapsed in 1911, the Republic that was formed and began seriously to absorb Western ideas and technologies was still distinctly Chinese.

The final terrible shock was partly external. The Japanese invasions, starting in 1927 and the declared Sino-Japanese war from 1937 to 1945, again killed millions and helped trigger another internal civil war between the Kuomintang government (KMT) and the Communists.

Then there were the thirty years in which Chairman Mao and the Communist Party tried to re-shape China from the bottom upwards. They tried to dig out the roots of the whole Confucian, relational, model and replace it with exact equality and communal property. The Cultural Revolution and the Great Leap Forward again led to the death of anything up to fifty million Chinese and appeared, for a time, to have abolished the old China. Yet we can now see that the old China is returning to ancient forms for its ancient forms from the liberalization in 1979 to the present.

How China expands

There are many other striking features of China. One is the way in which it has expanded. What we now call 'China' started over ten thousand years ago in the valley of the Yellow River, with civilisations which are only now being properly excavated. These spread and coalesced into the first full Chinese Empire in the second century BC. Since then China has relentlessly pushed outwards to its present shape. Yet China was not an Empire of the modern European kind. It was more like the Roman Empire, land rather than sea based. People settled in new areas, inter-married, turning people into Han.

The 'Middle Kingdom', as the Chinese called themselves, like the sun, had its circling planets, not fully incorporated but owing tribute and acceptance of China's superiority. Korea, Vietnam, Burma, Tibet, and at times Japan, circled with a gravitational pull from China. On the steppe borders China kept the nomads out by a mixture of walls, bribes and trade. So it never had a seaborne Empire, though the great early voyages to Africa and the Middle East show it could well have done so. Immense and complex waterways and a vast internal trade existed in China, larger in the seventeenth century than all the trade in the rest of the world combined. This may have turned the Chinese away from overseas adventures.

Though there have also been frequent sorties into neighbouring countries, these invasions never led, except in western China, to the permanent incorporation of the smaller states that surrounded it, such as Korea, Vietnam, Thailand, Burma or Nepal. This is a pattern which continues to this day, with the overseas Chinese energizing Africa, South America, Pakistan and many other places. It has no evangelical religion to spread, unlike Portugal, Spain or France. It has no desire to establish its laws and customs in the places it encounters and trades with, unlike the British Empire which took its laws and governmental system to underpin its trading.

Another shaping feature arises from the intersection of the geography and population. China early opted in the south for wet rice cultivation, combined with petty artisan work and trade. The population became very dense and, as with rice elsewhere, the cultivation method meant that human labour was very cheap and people worked incredibly hard.

Thrift, hard work, a desire for small profits from bi-occupations, are characteristic of thousands of years of Chinese civilisation. The Chinese are interested in money, they love gambling with it as well as saving it. All of this, with their hard, organized and collaborative work, lies behind the present immense economic boom and their success all over the world. They expect their children to work hard and achieve success in the new forms of economic activity, hence the brilliance of the pupils. They have long memories of the disasters of a famine-prone and highly precarious world where the weak and poor live where their noses were just above the water, easily drowned by periodic misfortunes.

The Chinese have most of the qualities which Max Weber saw as the 'puritan' ethic. Yet even with the character of thrifty, honest, ever-working, rational, 'puritans', it has only been in the last thirty years that real capitalism has arrived.

Belief, ritual and ethics

For a westerner, one of the most puzzling features of China is the pervasiveness of ritual, yet the absence of 'religion' in the western, single God, sense. In the west, we think of 'Religion' as being an institution where all of the major parts of a bundle are present – a Creator God, a dogma and set of beliefs about heaven, hell, sin, salvation, an ethical code, and a set of rituals by which we can approach and influence spiritual powers. If this total package is what we mean by 'religion', then none of the three major philosophies in China individually, or even when put together, constitute a 'Religion' as an autonomous and separate sphere.

Confucianism provides some ethics and social rituals, but no God or dogma about a spiritual world. Taoism has some rituals but no ethics or God. Buddhism has some rituals, ethics and some dogma but there is no creator God.

Another approach would be to argue that a phenomenon like 'religion' should be understood by setting up a set of possible features, and then seeing whether most of them (if not all) are present. If we do this, and include not only those noted above but also others, such as a belief in ghosts, the reverence due to ancestors, the power of certain sacred places or people, the sacredness of certain texts, then the Chinese have a 'family resemblance' to what we feel is 'religion' in the West.

Any visitor who has been to Shangri-La or the minority areas, or to the Confucian or Buddhist temples which are springing up in all their red and gold glory over China, will feel a sense of 'otherness'. We sense that some things are set apart from normal life, that people are aware of something larger than the individual, a power like electricity which runs through everything and hence requires geomancers to determine propitious days and directions.

So let us agree that, even before we allow for the now considerable presence of real religious sentiments in the minority areas (Tibetan Buddhism, Uighur Muslims) and now many Christians, China has many elements which seem roughly like certain aspects of religion in the West.

What it did not have was a dominant evangelical, proselytizing, monotheistic creed with its attendant vast corpus of priests, except for a short period in the Tang dynasty with Buddhism. Religion played little part in education, unlike in the West, and the religious did not form a separate order, like the Brahmins or clergy elsewhere.

There were no religious legal courts and apart from social ethics, religion was not a separate force in the economy or politics. The Emperor was heaven's representative and to be revered just as the father or husband was to be revered, but he was not a God.

What strikes a Westerner about China is how this-worldly and rational the Chinese are and have long been. To them, as with the Japanese, the huge influence of Judaism, Christianity or Islam in Western thought – in our philosophies, social life, even our economics and politics – is extraordinary. To them we seem very superstitious, God-soaked people. It is not surprising that, until recently, there has been no word for 'religion' in China. Even now, the word used, stresses veneration and obeying the rules of one's ancestors, rather than believing in a God. For many who live in the western world of fundamentalist conflicts, the heir to the Crusades and missionary endeavours, this can all seem refreshing, yet it has pervasive effects on China in many spheres.

Varieties of Buddhism

Two of the four civilisations I deal with here, China and Japan, have been heavily influenced by Buddhism. Yet the form of Buddhism which developed in these countries is very different indeed from that of India and South East Asia. It is a blend or hybrid and its mixed nature is one of the keys to understanding these far Eastern civilisations. In order to understand what happened, we need a first, basic, understanding of the central philosophies of Buddhism and an overview of its varieties, which I shall base on an article by Peter Pardue, from whom I quote.

According to widespread belief, the historical Buddha ("enlightened one"), Siddhārtha Gautama, was born a prince of an indigenous Indian clan in northern India about 550 B.C. At the age of 29 he left his home on his search for truth. Finally, in a single night of intensive meditation he achieved enlightenment and evolved his own unique diagnosis and teaching (Darma). It started as an oral tradition and none of the sayings of the Buddha were written down for some hundreds of years. Around the birth of Christ, the philosophy or religion split into two branches, and these later diverged into a third.

The first is the Theravāda ("teaching of the elders"), located in the lands of southeast Asia – most importantly in Ceylon, Burma, Thailand, Laos, Vietnam and Cambodia. The second is the Mahāyāna ("great vehicle"), in Nepal, Sikkim, China, Korea, and Japan. The third is the Tantrayāna ("esoteric vehicle"), formerly prevalent in Tibet, Mongolia, and parts of Siberia.

The Theravāda, as it exists today, represents the sole survivor of the numerous ancient Indian schools. It has a fixed body of canonical literature, a relatively unified orthodox teaching, a clearly structured institutional distinction between the monastic order and laity, and a long history as the established "church" of the various southeast Asian states. The Mahāyāna, on the other hand, is a diffuse and vastly complex combination of many schools and sects, based on a heterogeneous literature of massive proportions from which no uniform doctrinal or institutional orthodoxy can ever be derived. Institutionally it has appeared both in monastic and in radically laicized forms, and it has occasionally served in well-defined church-state configurations.

The main differences between Theravāda and Mahāyāna, which helped the latter to spread more widely and rapidly, are as follows. For the Theravāda, the Buddha was just a great teacher; for the Mahāyāna, he was divine. For the Theravāda, there was a considerable gap between the monks, who could attain Enlightenment and the laity, who could only partially attain it. For Mahāyāna, there was also the path of the Bodhisattva, someone who had accomplished this goal of becoming a 'fully enlightened Buddha', and yet had decided out of compassion to stay on earth and help ordinary people. This meant that the gap between the full-time monks and laity was diminished.

Thirdly, 'The missionary diffusion of Mahāyāna was greatly facilitated by a remarkable principle of rationalization which allowed for almost unlimited adaptability to given conditions. This was the idea of the Buddha's upāyakauśalya ('skill-in-means') – the ability to adjust teachings and institutions to the needs of all sorts and conditions of men through any means available.'

The third major division, which can also be seen as a part of Mahāyāna, was Tantric Buddhism, 'dominantly identified with Tibetan Lamaism and its theocracy, is equally ambiguous. The esoteric Tantric teachings, which originated in India, persisted in several so-called Mahāyāna schools in China and Japan. In its Tibetan form Tantric Buddhism was richly fused with a native primitivism, and it underwent important and very divergent sectarian developments.'

There are several central elements which are universal to Buddhism, however widely it differed across its huge area of influence.

First, for all Buddhists the common point of unity has been in the symbol of the Buddha – whether revered chiefly as a human teacher, as in Theravāda, or worshipped as a supreme deity, as in certain forms of theistic Mahāyāna. In all cases the element of personal commitment in faith is present in some form. Second, Buddhism is one of the three major religions of the world which defines the human situation with sufficient universality for all mankind to fall within the scope of its message of salvation without prior criteria of social, ethnic, or geographic origin. The voluntary act of personal conversion in response to the teaching was from the very beginning and still remains one of the most decisive symbols of its missionary scope. Third, from its very beginning Buddhism was dominated by a religious elite for whom the monastic ideal and pursuit of a mystical, other-worldly goal were overriding concerns, frequently to the exclusion of consistent focus on mundane socioeconomic and political problems.

The quintessence of the Buddha's teaching was encapsulated in the 'four noble truths', which can be summarised as follows.

1. All existence involves suffering.
2. The cause of suffering is desire (or attachment), because desire leads to rebirth.
3. The cessation of suffering can only be achieved through the cessation of desire.
4. The way of the Eightfold Path ends desire.

The way of release from the endless cycle of birth, death

and rebirth (*samsara*) and suffering and from *karma*, the inexorable moral law that dictates our fate in this cycle, is by way of the eightfold path, the first two and last two concerning achieving a correct state of mind, and the middle four to the correct conduct of life. The path is as follows.

1. Right outlook: to know the Four Noble Truths.
2. Right resolve: to overcome illusions caused by belief in an individual self.
3. Right speech: to refrain from untruth and frivolity.
4. Right conduct: to avoid harming living beings and to relieve suffering.
5. Right livelihood: to have an occupation in keeping with Buddhist precepts.
6. Right effort: to show determination to reach salvation.
7. Right mindfulness: to realize the dangers of discontents that arise from various physical and mental states.
8. Right concentration: to be free of distractions and illusions and to be alert and reflective.

In dealing with Buddhism, I am faced again with the difficulty of defining the border between a philosophy and a religion. People have argued about whether philosophies such as Confucianism, or ritual systems such as Daoism, are religions. It would appear that rather than being a single entity, religion is a package of features – ethics, beliefs, rituals – so that it is on a continuum. Some things are clearly full religions, others are part religion, part philosophy. Others are philosophies or sets of actions with a touch of religion. A hint of this is contained in an observation of the philosopher Alfred North Whitehead, who suggested that 'Christianity took the opposite road. It has always been a religion seeking a metaphysic, in contrast to Buddhism which is a metaphysic generating a religion.'

The philosophical core of China

A key to unlocking variations in philosophical and religious systems lies in an ideal of the philosopher Karl Jaspers. After he had studied the philosophies of many of the great classical thinkers from China to Europe, he suggested that they were all part of a great movement which he called the 'Axial Age'. He suggested that all the great civilisations of Eur-Asia went through a strangely parallel 'turning on their axes' about two and a half thousand years ago.

It is an idea which helps us to understand a great deal. The essence was the departure from a tribal world, where 'spirit' and invisible power was immanent, deeply interfused with this material world and everything around us, the kind of animistic shamanic world that I had come across in the Himalayan village where I spent many months as an anthropologist.

In such a world, there are practitioners who can put you in touch with the electric forces coursing through humans, animals, rocks and trees. Shamans go into trances and enter this parallel world and then come back to report what they have seen and heard. That kind of world had existed from very ancient times. It is one where there is no strong idea of an entirely separate 'heaven' or set of ideals against which we measure our lives.

Jaspers suggested that, roughly in a period of four hundred years (c. 800-400 B.C.), a number of great thinkers worked out a new philosophical system. Confucius, Mencius, Laotze, in China, the Buddha and the ancient Hindu scriptures in India, Zoroaster in Persia, the great old Testament prophets in the Middle East, and the great philosophers in Greece made a break.

They all suggested that there is this material world and there is an equally real 'ideal' order somewhere else and we need mediators, philosophers and religious experts, to bridge the two. In all cases the dogma and set of beliefs are to be written down in master texts which we should preserve and understand.

After he had studied the philosophies of Confucius the Buddha and Lao-Tzu (Lao-Tse) Karl Jaspers assumed that China, filled with three Axial philosophies, was part of the Axial transformation: 'the axial peoples are the Chinese, Indians, Iranians, Jews and Greeks'. On the other hand, Max Weber in his *Religion of China* argues that China was basically non-Axial, though he does not use that term. He describes it as a world where Confucius was not concerned with such a tension between this world and heaven, and Daoism created a magical and enchanted landscape from which the Chinese had not escaped.

It appears that there is a puzzle or contradiction. Perhaps the solution to this is that China is both Axial, and non-Axial at the same time. It may be that when the two great Axial philosophies, Confucian and Buddhist, came into conflict, and Buddhism also has to adapt to a very powerful set of pre-existing non-Axial beliefs – Daoism and Ancestor worship – then the effect is different from what we might expect.

Instead of there being a re-enforcement of Axiality, with each philosophy making the other more Axial, in fact they pulled against each other, so that the Axiality of both Confucianism and Buddhism was weakened in the new mix, and further weakened by Daoism, the third leg of the tripod as one Chinese Emperor put it. So China might be described as 'Axial-lite', perhaps a quarter of the way towards Axiality, and further weakened in its Axiality by the strength of the family and kinship system. The fact that Confucianism is, in itself, rather weakly Axial (Confucius was this-worldly, not much interested in Heaven) added to the peculiar situation in China.

As Buddhism evolved within China, it was deprived of some of its tension with another world, and incorporated into the animist world of Daoism. In this extreme form, it poses little threat to the State, it absorbs a good deal of Daoism, and it forms no threat to Confucianism. It is similar in many ways to western Puritanism in being a simple, ascetic, inward-looking, private system, where salvation is by faith rather than works, through inner cleansing and meditation. Yet, in contrast to Christian sects, it does not have God. This difference would have a profound effect on many parts of Chinese development, including the progress of reliable knowledge ('science') in China.

Technology and science in China

The great scholar of Chinese science and civilisation, Joseph Needham, spent the later part of his life documenting, in a series of massive volumes, the sophistication and precocity of Chinese technology. By the fourteenth century the Chinese had invented most of the great technologies in the world – mechanical clocks, mechanical weaving, gunpowder, the compass, printing, porcelain, silk weaving, tea cultivation, complex irrigation systems, huge boats with internal air devices to keep boats afloat, and an extraordinary educational system based on merit.

If anywhere was likely to break through into an industrial, scientific, kind of world, an observer looking back to the time when Marco Polo in the thirteenth century visited the largest city in the world, Hangzhou, might have predicted that it would be China.

Yet not only did China not develop in this way, hitting what Mark Elvin has called the 'high-level equilibrium trap', but it became weaker, at least relatively, so that by the nineteenth century the richest and most ancient civilisation in the world was humiliated by Britain. This is particularly astonishing in that even until the middle of the nineteenth century, the majority of the world's wealth was in China.

Why was this? There are many contending theories and, as we shall see, any explanation will have to recognise that perhaps the problem, which also applies to the glories of Islamic civilisation up to the twelfth century, needs to be posed in a different way. For, as Adam Smith recognised, China was normal in hitting a ceiling, just as all the great Mediterranean countries had also halted. The move to a new industrial world ultimately only happened in one small part of the world.

The basis of the arduous pursuit of the natural laws which are believed to lie behind the surface of life, as we can see in the life of a Newton or Einstein, or earlier of Roger Bacon or Galileo, is the belief that there are stable principles, recurring patterns, to be discovered. It is believed that the universe can be understood at a deeper level. The Creator God, the great clockmaker, had started the machine and it ran on its way according to His laws. He had encouraged his human creation to find out how it worked by systematic enquiry.

Just as a child finds out how the world works by hypothesis, 'it may be hot', and testing, lightly touching an object, so scientists proceed on the basis of conjecture, refutations, confirmations and proof. They make repeated tests which are worth making if nature and its deeper laws are believed to be constant and the experiments can be repeated. None of the major philosophies of China gave this kind of experimental search for invariable laws an impetus.

The Confucians were not interested in finding out such laws, even though they might seek 'the way' (dao). They were mainly concerned with social and political ethics and were rather disdainful of the practical, demeaning, economic world.

Like the Daoists, they lived in a magical universe filled with forces which were incomprehensible and only mildly controllable. There was no point in trying to systematise and investigate, beyond a surface understanding of certain relations and symbols.

The Buddhists were even less interested in such an endeavour, for they suggested a world where what we experience is ultimately an illusion, 'maya'. All that is around us and seems 'real' will disappear when we reach true enlightenment. So there is little point in trying to understand or change this set of external shadows. Our task is to make the shadows evaporate.

Furthermore, we live in a completed world in China. We inherit the great wisdom of the founding Fathers, Confucius, Laotze, Mencius and the Buddha. They mapped out all that we need to know. We must just preserve, and at the most expand a little, of their vision.

By the sixteenth century, but only in Europe, there had emerged a progressive science which separated that civilisations from all others, an experimental and systematic technology for the manufacture of detailed knowledge about the world's working which could then be applied, through rapidly changing technology, to the material world.

What China is and will be

It is now difficult to see what the situation is. Because of the amazing economic, technological, social, political and cultural changes of the last thirty years, a series of rapid and huge changes unparalleled in the history of the world, especially in such a short and peaceful way, there is much confusion. It is not easy to discern whether the deep structure has been destroyed, damaged, or merely overlain, waiting to be revived.

My guess is that when historians look back on the current period in a hundred years' time, as we can look back on the Manchus or the Opium Wars, they will conclude that, while the surface and certain elements may have changed hugely, the basic relational, structure has remained.

I have quizzed my younger Chinese friends about this problem, dazed by how fast their life and lifestyles are changing every day so that they tell me that they cannot understand people two or three years older or younger than themselves. I sense that while they feel very different from their parents, especially if they have been partially educated abroad, they quickly revert to the previous patterns as they grow older and especially if they return to live in China. They feel at one with other Chinese, and like to be with them and linked to them.

One reason for believing that China will remain the old China is because of China's immense bulk. It is like some great ocean liner which gets buffeted by gales and waves but ploughs on. Even Chairman Mao could not destroy or redirect it at a deep level. Currently much of China's effort is to integrate useful outside things while paying increasing attention to the revival of the vast and valuable legacy of its ancient linguistic, artistic, cultural and social traditions.

China could be seen to lead the way. Its ancient and magnificent art, culture, technology and wealth were unparalleled up to the early nineteenth century. It lacked many of the disfiguring features of other worlds. China was often peaceful and in general less aggressive than western civilisations. The philosophy put a high premium on harmonious social relations. It was highly literate and respectful of knowledge. The Chinese people were, and are, hard-working, tolerant and rational, ingenious and humorous. In many respects it was not just the longest and largest civilisation in history, but the most estimable.

Lacking religious fundamentalism, striving to adapt to its ecology and environment to make a living for millions in an often difficult world, it has created a model for all of us. Now that we face the Chinese century ahead, with Chinese food, culture and people spreading very widely, it provides an alternative to various aggressive fundamentalisms elsewhere. Yet if we are to benefit from its lessons, we need to understand it.

People often ask me about the future of China, as I see it as a sympathetic outsider. There are certain things which seem likely to happen; probabilities are all that one can deal with in such an attempt at prophecy.

The first thing that seems pretty certain is that China will endure. It has survived myriad attacks and revolutions and recovered. The present turmoils – huge growth and redistributions and scientific, technological, educational and other changes – though they look like something that would break a civilisation are being dealt with.

China went through the huge changes of industrialization and urbanization in a generation, while the British achieved this in over a period of three generations. Yet the Chinese case has, in terms of the speed and size of what has happened, caused much less disruption, poverty, brutality and pollution relative to the size of the two populations. It was far faster and affected a population ten times the size of the other comparable industrial revolutions of Japan and Britain.

If China can cope with the urban and industrial revolution in this way and not fall apart, there is no reason to think it will do so in the future. It has gone through the huge trauma of leaving an agrarian world and now is sailing on calmer water, even though it faces other problems. Built on the structural cohesiveness which I described earlier, China is immensely tough, extendable and efficient. It will survive and grow. My guess is that China has only reached a small part of its potential and that in thirty years it will be (again) the most important economy and civilisation on the planet – reaching out and influencing lives all over this world.

As far as I can see, while it wants to create a reasonable life for its citizens, and also would like others to understand and appreciate its great traditions, it has no missionizing zeal to make others 'Chinese'. There is no interest in turning us all into Taoist, Confucian, Communists, Buddhists, Mandarin-speakers or lovers of Beijing opera.

Here it is different from the Spanish, French, British, American, civilisations which tried to make all those it encountered conform to themselves – whether this was Christianity, capitalism, human rights or western-style democracy. China does not, and has never, believed that others can be forced to change their culture at the point of a sword or with a gun. Even if they were to be 'converted', what is it to? Playing mah jong, drinking tea, appreciating the Ancient classics, calligraphy, a respect for parents and authority? This is the limit of the package to be exported.

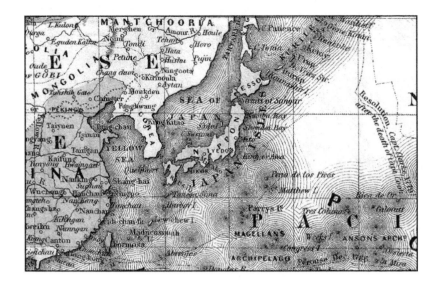

The Japanosphere

MY INVOLVEMENT WITH Japan started by accident. In early 1990 the British Council invited me to become a Visiting Scholar in Japan. The Council wished to send out a British academic to spend a month or two in Japan to give a few lectures and establish contacts. I learnt that the official invitation had come from a Professor Kenichi Nakamura in the Law Faculty at Hokkaido University. I later learnt he had been urged to invite me because his wife Toshiko had been interested by a book I had written on love and marriage in England. I was also intrigued, for I had read about the northern Ainu and wanted to visit them. Furthermore, in my reading I had encountered similarities between England and Japan. I accepted the invitation.

I knew little about Japan before our first visit. It was, I

assumed, more or less a small version of China. I believed that for much of its history Japan had used roughly the same language, had similar art and aesthetics, a similar family system, a similar religion (Buddhist, Confucian), a similar agriculture and diet (rice, tea), similar architecture and that both had an Emperor system. Only recently had the two diverged, China becoming a communist, Japan a capitalist society.

I knew Japan to be an ultra-modern and efficient country, home to more than a hundred million people. It was the first industrial nation in Asia by more than two generations and the second largest economy in the world when I visited it for the first time. It seemed, from afar, the epitome of a modern, capitalist, scientific society, a country with incredibly large cities, hard workers, efficient transport systems, sophisticated arts and crafts. It was famous for its engineering and electronics.

If I had been asked to set up a balance sheet of my pre-conceptions, it might have read as follows. The positive side included the beautiful arts and crafts; wonderful gadgets; exquisite temples and gardens; a samurai culture of honour; tea ceremony and ethic; intriguing games and arts including *sumo* wrestling and *kabuki* theatre. The negative included the behaviour of the Japanese military in the Second World War; violent suicide; organized crime and the *yakuza*; over-conformity; pollution and urban blight; violent pornography.

Such was the distorted and confused picture I had when, at the age of forty-eight, I embarked with my wife Sarah for Japan. The first visit was wonderful and I was keen to go back to find out more. So we continued to visit the country every two or three years for the next twenty years, making eight trips in all, including three months teaching at Tokyo University. We became very close friends with several Japanese, particularly Toshiko and Kenichi Nakamura who guided us through the complexities of the difficult world of Japan. We tried to understand each other's cultures over the fifteen years before I wrote *Japan Through the Looking Glass* (2007) which was, in effect, jointly written with them.

Language and aesthetics

In Japan there are indeed many features that derive from China. Yet, as we shall see, in each case the borrowing is subverted by the Japanese so that, as any particular feature crosses the hundred miles of stormy seas and is filtered through Japanese sensibility, it is radically changed.

At first sight the language, with its use of thousands of Chinese characters (*kanji*), which all Japanese children spend half their schooldays learning, seems to be identical. It is pictographic or logographic. Yet then we notice that in order to inflect and modify it the Japanese have added two syllabaries, *katakana* and *hiragana*. By doing this, and by modifying the symbols in accordance with Japanese thought, the deeper language – the grammar, syntax, semantics – is entirely different from Mandarin Chinese.

Chinese grammar is almost interchangeable with English; Japanese language, whose origin is still obscure, is totally different from English or any other language. Many believe it is so flexible, imprecise, without tenses, without the use of personal pronouns, a curious word order, the absence of positive and negative, words that have multiple meanings, that it is impossible to say anything definite in it. Indeed, as the Japanese proverb goes,' language is a barrier to communication'. I have seen this in my encounters with Japanese friends. They often have enormous difficulty in translating a piece of Japanese for me, while my Chinese friends have no such difficulty. Essentially Chinese and Japanese are as far apart as English and Hindi.

A second impression might be that the aesthetics are more or less identical. Visiting Kyoto does not at first feel so different from visiting some old Chinese cities with their temples and shrines. There is the same love of red and gold; the apparently similar shapes of the shrines and buildings and courtyards; the use of rock and trees in gardens.

Yet, if one probes deeper, there are again immense differences. Putting it very simply, the Chinese love regularity, paired oppositions, two and four and eight. The symmetry of the rings of the Forbidden City is archetypical. Beauty lies in balance and harmony between equal parts. It is like classical Greece or Rome.

In Japan it is the opposite. Balance, symmetry, harmony of that kind is oppressive and boring. It is the productive tension of unbalanced features, of the numbers three and nine, of five teacups, never six, that rests the mind and allows it to expand. Things should be rough and allusive, unfinished, as with the twisting paths, the rough tea-houses, the apparently half-baked but hugely valuable tea bowls. It is a world of shadows and mysteries. The difference between a rough, blackened, Japanese tea bowl and an amazing, satin-finished, Chinese porcelain cup sums it up.

The whole relation between representation and reality is different. Japan is a country of miniaturization – tiny trees (*bonsai*), miniature gardens, tiny carved objects (*netsuke*), tiny gestures. Each one stands for a far greater reality generated by the mind, adding water to the powder of the tiny symbol. All is about simplicity, making things as small and elegant as possible, reduced to its elements. A single flower or rock can stand for a world.

There is something of this in China too, but generally things are on a much larger and more direct scale. The rock gardens and the buildings are bigger and life-size. The oldest opera, such as the *Kunqu* is less allusive than Japanese *Noh* drama. There is not the same intense compression we see in Japan. There is little in China directly equivalent to the simplest of poetic forms a *haiku*.

Race

Another way in which we might be led to believe that these two Mongoloid peoples are roughly the same is in terms of race. Yet there are huge differences. Most Chinese are a mixture of the Han of central China with waves of migration from the inland tribes and the indigenous ethnic minority groups. There is great diversity but also a great deal of uniformity.

Recent research on Japanese DNA and culture suggests that the Japanese comprise at least four major and very different groups. There are traces of the original inhabitants, a Caucasian race called the Ainu, of whom only a few 'pure' individuals remain in the northern island of Hokkaido. The northern parts are also heavily colonized by people who came down from the Korean peninsula and who are connected with peoples from the Altaic mountains on the Siberian border.

In the middle there is predominantly a different group who probably came across from the nearest landmass, China. Then, in the south, on Kyushu and the islands which lie like a chain below Japan, are people who migrated up from further south, Pacific Islanders with more affinities to the Philippines, Malaysia and that area. So when you sit on a Japanese subway you see people whose faces are enormously varied in colour and shape, much more so than in China.

Material culture

Another area where a first glance might suggest similarity

is in food and drink. Both countries seem to be until recently mainly vegetarian, though the Chinese also ate some duck and pig, and much of the cooking revolves around rice. Yet even the way rice is cooked is different – in China it is usually dried out, in Japan very often left sticky.

The way of cooking and the flavouring is not the same. As the saying goes, Japanese food is 'eaten with the eye', for it is often served very beautifully. Yet if you eat it in the dark, it has only the subtlest of flavours. Chinese, like Indian food, is eaten with the stomach, and is equally tasty in dim light. Chinese food also becomes spicy as one moves towards the south-west. In terms of drink there is again both similarity and difference. Neither culture traditionally drank a great deal of alcohol, but the *sake* of Japan is not the same as the rice wines of China.

As for the national drink of both, tea, there is both similarity and difference. Both enjoy green tea, but the powdered green tea of Japan (*macha*) is hardly known in China and the brown and black teas of China are much less frequent in Japan. The tea ceremony of Japan is derived from the Chinese Tang tea ceremony, but has been preserved and elaborated into something rather different. So the present day tea ceremony of China is relatively simple and speedy, pouring hot water over miniature cups and teapots, percolation, serving and drinking. In Japan, there are elaborate teahouses, tea mistresses, short and long ceremonies often taking up to several hours, enormously elaborate etiquette and conversation. Learning to be a tea master or mistress can take a lifetime.

Again the traditional housing might at first strike outsiders as similar – houses made of simple materials with little use of stone, much use of bamboo, no foundations, paper windows, elegant toilets. Yet the feel of a Chinese country house and a Japanese one is totally different. The Chinese house has a solidity and a prosaic utility. Most traditional Chinese houses are more substantial than those of Japan, especially in the colder north. There the Chinese house with its heated bed (*kang*) and large frying bowl (*wok*) for cooking in oil, feels very unlike the 'paper lanterns' of Japanese houses, until recently built like tents to deal with the frequent earthquakes. The Japanese houses in cities and towns were very cheap as they tended to go up in flames on average every twelve years or so.

Japanese homes have 'sacred' areas, the tatami matting room, perhaps with a small ancestor box (*butsudan*) and recess with a scroll and special rough object (*tokonoma*). In all parts of the house except the kitchen area, shoes must be taken off. Although traditionally Chinese houses often had ancestor boxes or tablets, in China this custom of shoe removing is not nearly as pronounced. Another fundamental difference for at least a thousand years is that while the Japanese lived at floor level, sitting and lying on mats, the Chinese used chairs, tables and beds.

In terms of clothing, again there are great differences. The clothing of the majority of Japanese was very similar in the past, with men and women more or less wearing identical simple cotton clothes. They had either straw or wooden sandals or shoes and feet should never touch the earth. In portraits and accounts of pre-twentieth century China, we see that many people went barefoot, but the use of silk for the wealthy was on a far larger scale. Of course another huge difference was that for half a millennium the custom of foot- binding of women was widespread in China, but was never exported to Japan.

It would be possible to continue noting some overlap but also huge differences in the material world – the absence of the Chinese wheelbarrow and indeed of all wheels traditionally in Japan, the absence of pigs and ducks in Japan and so on. Even the disease patterns were different – China suffered again and again from major diseases, particularly bubonic plague. Japan was free of almost all endemic and epidemic diseases except smallpox and later cholera.

Power and administration

While the material and physical worlds on the small rocky islands of Japan and the huge landmass of China were contrasted enough, it is when we come to the social, philosophical and political that extraordinary differences really emerge.

On first view, the Chinese and Japanese political and administrative systems in the past might seem quite similar. After all, both countries had an imperial system, with the Emperor living surrounded by his court in a 'forbidden city'. Furthermore, the governmental system of Japan in the seventh to ninth centuries, the Nara and Heian period, was explicitly modeled on the Tang Chinese system, even down to the court music (*gagaku*) which survives to this day in Japan, whereas it became almost extinct in China.

Or again the philosophy behind the administration of both was supposedly Confucian, with its duty to superiors, whether family or Emperor. Again, the power of the administration and of the family system was such that legal institutions, lawyers, law courts, legal training centres, developed civil codes, were hardly to be found over much of the history of either civilisation.

Yet the surface similarities largely evaporate when we look closer. The great difference lies in the fact that Japan threw off most of its Chinese mantle in the twelfth century, the Kamakura period. It built up instead a centralised feudal system, almost identical, incidentally, to the English political system of that period. China on the other hand had become a bureaucratic, civil, administrative state more than a thousand years before.

The Japanese ruled through a system of contractual, feudal, downward delegation of power and responsibility; the Emperor, the *daimyo* and their samurai retainers, and then the peasants, all holding estates from their superiors in the feudal chain. Each provided their superiors with services, loyalty and some rents in return for their estates. This was the system found in early China about three thousand years ago in the Zhou dynasty. Yet as we have seen it was replaced by the Qin over two thousand years ago with a Mandarin system, based on educational qualifications. In Japan there was an armed ruling nobility, in China a civil bureaucracy.

This huge difference was also reflected in the division of power at the centre of the system. The Chinese had one apex, the Emperor, on whom all power was centred. In Japan, for a thousand years, power was split between the military ruler, the Shogun, residing in Kamakura or Tokyo, and the ceremonial ruler, the Emperor, in Kyoto. This split reminds one of the monarchy and parliament in Britain, for many centuries a balance between ceremonial head and an executive branch. There was a balance of power, a productive tension which was a source of potential openness. This was very different from the unified Chinese system.

Again, when we examine the philosophy underpinning these systems the surface resemblances disappear. The Japanese took the Confucian conflation of political allegiance to one's superior, whether daimyo or samurai, and social allegiance to one's father. Yet they reversed the primary allegiance. In China, the father came first; you should kill the Emperor rather than kill your father. In Japan the primary allegiance was to the political power; if necessary, you killed your father rather than the Emperor.

This may not at first seem a huge difference, for few would

be faced with the choice in practice. Yet it is the fundamental shift to a world where politics, based on non-blood, contractual, relationships comes before blood-based 'status'. It is one of the essential features of the transition from 'status' to 'contract', which is the key to what Sir Henry Maine called the 'progressive societies'. It leads to a disembedding of politics and a weakening of the blood family.

Family system

Many observers have assumed that the Chinese and Japanese family systems are roughly the same. After all, we know that both have clans, or groups of relatives, we know that the wider family has been very important, with arranged marriages of a kind and children very dependent on and emotionally close to their parents.

Yet again, below the surface, there are immense differences in every respect. In terms of how people think of, and address, their relatives, the two systems are totally opposed. The Chinese system is based on differentiating male and female lines and tracing one's ancestry and using kinship terms based exclusively on the male line. The Japanese trace their ancestry through both males and females and hence do not form into bounded groups. The Japanese kinship terminology starts with an individual and forms rings of parents and siblings, uncles and aunts, cousins, nephews and nieces. It is exactly the same as that of the Anglosphere, and it is totally different from that of China.

Another crucial feature is that of inheritance. Here the two systems could not be more contrasted. In China all children are automatically born into the family property, the daughters receive dowries, the sons automatically share the land and housing. It is a partible, multiple heir, inheritance system where the parents are really trustees of a joint property. There is little possibility of disinheriting a child, no possibility of adopting in non-blood relative to replace one's blood heirs. There is no possibility of making a will to leave one's property to others outside the family.

In Japan, as in England for nearly a thousand years, the property can be divided as one likes, although in richer families the central property should not be split into pieces. All the assets are the private property of the parents and, ideally, the bulk of it should be passed on by them to just one heir. This fits with a feudal system where it was in the Lord's interest that his retainers had reasonable sized holdings from which they could send armed supporters when needed.

In Japan, if no suitably talented heir exists, anyone can be adopted, blood relatives or strangers. This happens not only in the inheritance of land but also of businesses, crafts and cultural skills. You find it among *kabuki* actors, *sumo* wrestlers and university professors.

The result is that the Chinese have a powerful, blood-based, patrilineal (descent through males) clan system, forming the pivot of the social structure. In the past whole villages in certain parts of China consisted of one out-marrying clan – the Wangs, the Li's, the Xu's or whatever. This did not happen in Japan, where the families are artificial, each child potentially, as in England, in a position where they can be ejected from the succession.

This does not mean that family sentiments are unimportant in Japan. In fact the family-like, quasi- kinship, feelings become generalized so that many organisations in Japan, whether a business, factory, school, artistic establishment or even the army 'feel' like a sort of extended family. Yet these are a mixture of contractual relations and birth-based sentiments, a stronger version of what you may find in some Anglosphere clubs and associations.

Japan has something not dissimilar to a 'civil society', of constructed communities. Such artificial entities, based on choice mixed with family-like sentiment, have proliferated in Japan, as they have in the Anglosphere. Civil society is very different and difficult to generate in China where the family has been an undivided building block until the middle of the twentieth century. Over the last three generations, however, the family has been partly atomized, firstly by the attempt of Chairman Mao to break the hold of the clan, and now increasingly by a more individualistic education system, market economy and new legal rights, all of which are rapidly decreasing the power of parents and the wider family.

In the same realm of the family lie gender and sex relations. A strong feature of the Confucian system, as we have seen in China, is the birth-based superiority of men: all women are below men and in extreme cases, women have to be protected from other men by seclusion and foot binding. Although there is also a traditional inbuilt inferiority in Japan, so that a brother is superior to a sister and a woman has to address men in a special, deferential, language, in general there is a greater equality of the sexes. Women were active in all spheres in traditional Japan. They were the greatest writers, sometimes famed warriors, in charge of domestic finances, presiding over the house as *O-kami-san* (honourable 'god' lady). There was, as everywhere in Japan, structural inequality, yet it was not as great as people often imagine.

Sex and the body

The attitude towards the human body, and in particular to its sexual attributes and functions, is very contrasted in China and Japan. In all that I have observed on my frequent visits to China there is a great similarity to the older mixture of innocence and puritanism that I remember in the England of my childhood after the Second World War.

It is true that in China the body is not a source of sin or dangerous temptation, as in the Christian West, but it is also to be treated with modesty and decorum. It should be reasonably covered, not provocatively dressed, and all overt sexual gestures, especially kissing in public, should be avoided. There is no question of open nudity, whether in public baths or hot springs, and there is only a peripheral pornographic literature and art.

All this is at a distance from the curious contradictions of Japanese sexual attitudes. On the one hand there is a similar innocence, combined with prudishness – kissing in public was again absolutely taboo. Yet the innocence and non-sexuality is taken much further so that the naked body, as in mixed or single sex naked bathing, is not considered innately wrong. The Japanese innocence was all quite shocking to early Western missionaries.

In total contradiction, however, Japan is also famous for its extreme pornography and sex entertainment industry. The graphic 'pillow' books, the prostitute quarters in the big cities, the courtesan world of the *geisha*, all these are part of a world where sex is seen as a guilt-free and natural process, on a par with eating or drinking.

The huge differences between Japan and China can lead to tragic misunderstanding, as in the treatment of local Chinese and Korean women by the Japanese troops during the Second World War. The expectations and morality clashed hugely and many Japanese can still not understand the anger and desire for apologies of Chinese and Koreans at the treatment of the 'comfort women'. The whole history of Sino-Japanese relations between 1927 and 1945 is filled with the most ghastly events which still lead to fierce denunciations and rebuttals.

Inter-connectedness

I described the Chinese as 'structural' peoples, who have their meaning in relation to others. No single Chinese, father or child, subject or ruler, has much individual meaning. It is a group, or pair-based, civilisation. This is also true of the Japanese, who exist in their relations and not separately. The Zen proverb about the sound of one hand clapping (unimaginable) captures this. Here Japan and China are alike, but beyond this there are some curious differences.

On the one hand, the alignment with others, the degree of interdependence, is much greater in Japan. If China seems to be a place of partial separation, where Yin and Yang are paired facets, like sun and moon or night and day, separate but needing each other to have meaning, the blending or interrelatedness of the Japanese is much more intense.

The well-known image that captures this is the '*natto*' society (*natto* are fermented bean sprouts). The beans put out little tendrils, which intertwine with the others into an inseparable mass or blob of thousands of shoots. This is a way of thinking of the Japanese. Each person is entwined with every other Japanese they meet, owing them honour and respect, filled with an internal obligation of gratitude or '*on*', a debt which can never be repaid.

Of course this '*on*' is strongest to parents who gave one the gift of life. Yet it is also felt in relation to everyone else, teachers, co-workers, bosses, political leaders and even strangers. Consequently many people believe that this interdependent mass feeling of the Japanese must leave them with no individuality. People are totally absorbed into each other with no boundaries. This seems to be expressed in the complete banning of the use of personal pronouns. You should not use the word 'I', though it exists in Japanese, and so you are forced into circumlocutions that have to be used to refer to yourself, looked at from the outside and through other's eyes.

Yet, curiously, such is the interdependence that it leads into great loneliness and self-doubt. The famous 'I' novels of the early 20th century explored this. The metaphor of Japanese society as being like a set of lobster pots on a rope, each inhabited by a single lobster unable to communicate with others; the extraordinary phenomenon of the 'shut away children', several hundred thousand young people who spend years locked away in their bedrooms refusing to come out; the high rates of suicide as a result of feeling totally cut off society, all these are signs of this inner loneliness.

So my experience with many Chinese and Japanese students and friends over the years, and of watching people on our visits to both China and Japan, is that the Chinese are gregarious, love to spend time with their Chinese friends, chatter away, feel easy and equal in meeting new strangers. The Japanese often avoid each other – especially abroad – sit for long periods in silence. My Japanese students continue to treat me with formal respect and deference over the years, insisting on calling me 'sensei' (teacher). My Chinese students and friends soon adopt my personal name and treat me as almost equal.

Some would put this down to early childrearing. Certainly in Japan the closeness between mother and child, leading into what has been called the amae (dependence) complex is very notable. Infants were traditionally 'glued' to their mothers for a number of years. There was very long breastfeeding, children had to be carried all the time, they slept with their parents on the tatami matting through the first five or more years. They were hardly separated and remain deeply entwined with their parents for life.

There is only some of this in China. For what I have

observed is far less extreme. Young toddlers I have seen in the streets of China are often on their own, they are not carried everywhere, they are not necessarily sleeping in the same bed as their parents.

Purity and danger

One obsession of the Japanese is with what anthropologists call 'purity and danger'. Space and time are sharply divided so that the 'clean' and the 'unclean', the outer and inner, the higher and the lower, are kept apart as much as possible. This can be seen in the immaculate cleanliness of the houses and streets and subway stations (every matchstick is carefully swept up) and even of the fields in traditional Japan. It can be seen in the care with which outer garments, soiled in contact with general 'dirt', had to be shed when entering a house or shrine, particularly one's shoes, and even within a house there are special slippers for use in the 'polluted' bathroom.

All this reminds me a little of the extreme forms of puritan, Dutch, cleanliness in the age of Rembrandt, but is much more extreme. It is different from China where an obsession with purity and cleanliness is largely absent. The reputation for dirtiness which the Chinese gained in the nineteenth century, spitting in the street, carts carrying human feces away, pigs and ducks leaving their excrement around, objects thrown into public spaces, was much exaggerated. Certainly on our visits we have been impressed by the level of cleanliness equal to that in Britain. Yet there is not the Japanese obsession.

The difference can be seen also in one curious phenomenon. Not many people know that while Japan does not have a system based on ritual purity similar to the caste system in India, it does have, in the past, one 'untouchable' and outcaste group – the *burakamin* or, in the most derogatory styling, the '*eta*' (or 'non-people').

This group of several millions, mainly in central Japan, have existed for at least half a millennium but has been kept largely secret from outsiders, but known to the Japanese. They are the people involved in the butchery of animals, leather working, certain crafts. Their work turns nature into culture and is linked to blood and death. By an extraordinary turn, these most polluted of people – no Japanese should marry or take food from them – are those who traditionally carry the dead Emperor's coffin. The purest, the Emperor, becomes polluted by death and is carried through the streets at his funeral by them. There is nothing like this in China.

Nationalism

Japan is a large island, surrounded by dangerous seas. Like Britain, but on a much grander and more intense scale, it has been both insular and nationalist. With constant waves of immigration and only twenty miles of fairly calm sea dividing Britain from the Continent, the British were somewhat watered down in their xenophobia and despising of foreigners. Yet certainly at times of danger, or at the height of their empire, there was an arrogance and intolerance.

This is carried to a greater extreme in Japan. Traditionally, if a Japanese sailor was lost at sea and later returned to Japan, he was killed. Foreign traders for some centuries were not allowed to visit the mainland, but held in a buffer zone, a 'decontamination chamber', on Deshima island in Nagasaki bay. Until recently, those Japanese who spent a few years abroad and returned to Japan were considered to have lost their 'Japaneseness'. More recently, foreigners who settled in Japan, who spoke fluent Japanese, perhaps married a Japanese husband or wife, were never allowed to feel anything but *gaijin*, foreigners.

At its extreme, when Japan was at its strongest and re-arranged its classification of peoples in the later nineteenth century, this made foreigners, including Chinese, basically inferior, semi-barbarians, only semi-human. There is great gentleness and sensitivity and aesthetic sensibility among many individual Japanese. Yet this is combined with their notorious treatment of prisoners and enemies in war. They behave as if they are dealing with animals rather than humans. This is largely explained by their long isolation and the way they classify others.

The Japanese combine great deference when weak, with arrogance and brutality when strong. This was noted by their two great social philosophers of modern times, Fukuzawa Yukichi and Murayama Masao. The aim of the Japanese was to seal off the island, to repel dangerous and polluted visitors, and if they encountered others, to decide whether to treat them as superior (to whom one should abase oneself), as they did for long periods to the Chinese and more recently the Americans, or as inferiors, with little common human bond.

All of this contrasts with what I have seen of China. It is true that proud westerners were often treated with disdain on their trade missions to the Chinese Emperors in the eigh-teenth century, or missionaries and others in the nineteenth. Confident in their knowledge that the Middle Kingdom was the centre of the world, the oldest, greatest, most civilised and self-sufficient of worlds, some Chinese were at times com-placently self-confident. There was an attitude we find with all great Imperial powers, whether the Romans, British or Americans. We are civilised, they are the barbarians.

Yet this general complacency did not turn into xenophobia or desire to shut off all communications and to treat the peoples they encountered as non-human. Rather, on the contrary, the Chinese hoped to trade, settle, intermarry, to turn those on the edge into Chinese. China was an expanding sponge, not a rocky fortress like Japan. Anyone who wanted to be 'Chinese' was welcome to be so. At the extreme this included the marauding Mongols and Manchus, who had slain millions of Han, but who soon became Chinese and are now considered to be among the ancestors of the current population.

Thus while the Japanese almost exterminated the large aboriginal population, the Ainu, the Chinese rejoice in the fact that there are a hundred million ethnic minority peoples, many of whom have been given semi-autonomous rule and are encouraged to keep their customs and costumes as long as they do not threaten the political sovereignty of the Empire and now the Party.

Classes and cities

Another enormous difference lies in the arrangement and constitution of the social strata in Japan and China. As we have seen, China after the end of feudalism two thousand years ago had a structure – the *literati*, bureaucracy, Imperial system on top, and the rest. This two level structure, which placed peasants above merchants and craftsmen, is very simple and powerful. It allowed no place for a military nobility, an autonomous bourgeoisie, or a clerical group.

Japan has a fourfold stratification system which might at first seem to make it fit with the four Indo-European orders (nobles and military rulers, clergy and notaries, bourgeoisie, peasants). Yet the Japanese hierarchy was really very different from that in the West and also China.

It completely lacked the clerical order of Indo-Europe; there was nothing equivalent to Brahmins, mullahs or Christian priests. So one might imagine that there would be just three orders, but there are in fact four. This was because the huge importance of the economy in Japan was reflected in there being two 'bourgeois' groups, the merchants and the manufacturers (artisans). Both were placed below the peasants in order of precedence, yet both were enormously important.

Behind this lay another difference. Economic success in making things and in trading was not disparaged in Japan as greedy and demeaning, but highly esteemed. Large trading and manufacturing organisations have existed in Japan for hundreds of years and later turned into firms like Mitsui and Mitsubishi, Sony and Honda.

Much of this activity spread all over Japan, with its good coastal communications. Much of the activity took place within cities which again, although sometimes looking as if they were based on Chinese models, had an entirely contrasted feel.

Chinese cities were fortresses, with no separate legal or cultural existence, just places for the administration, for fairs and markets. The great cities of Japan, Osaka, Kyoto, Kamakura, Edo (Tokyo) and others developed their own life and culture. They were not seen as threatening or to be crushed by the political powers. A feudal system of power, which allowed a similar development of autonomous and independent cities in the West, encouraged city growth in both parts of the world.

So the Japanese became superb manufacturers, their objects beautifully crafted for a discriminating internal market and later taking the world by storm. They could, like the Chinese, imitate anything presented to them and their obsession with miniaturization made them particularly successful in a world that moved towards the 'micro'.

Making money and expressing it in modest consumption was honourable and not dangerous. Dynasties and firms continued over the generations, recruiting on a semi-family model, to their estate or businesses the most talented who were treated as the heirs but were often adopted strangers.

The fourfold Japanese social order was purely based on function, an 'organic' solidarity where each level played its part. Mobility between these was not too difficult. They were classes and not castes, and there were many tales of younger sons having to leave home and becoming rich entrepreneurs in the cities and starting their own successful line. The path of social mobility in China was totally contrasted. To move right to the top was possible, but only, basically, through intellectual aptitude and a good deal of luck.

Education and religion

The education systems of Japan and China overlap. There is a similar Confucian esteem for learning, a large concentration on language and literature, widespread literacy in the immensely complex logograms and syllabaries. There is a high regard for the classics, for poetry, novels and autobiographies. Both have great compilations of classical works and a vast output of books.

Yet, while education was the ladder in China and directed primarily to the brain, in Japan education was important but different. The ruling class in Japan was not composed of civil bureaucrats but armed soldiers, daimyo and samurai. So schooling had something of the feel of a toughening up for Imperial service in the Army, Navy or Empire of the traditional British boarding system. It was more about martial arts, endurance and character than the Chinese system.

Yet in both there was a notable absence of professional training for other occupations – no legal, clerical, little medical or other professional education. In both the emphasis was away from rhetorical, logical, mathematical emphases of the higher parts of western education.

The absence of a central and instituted clerical class (though, of course, both China and Japan had monastic traditions within Buddhism which trained monks) takes us to perhaps the most important of the deep differences. Both China and Japan were ancient civilisations, though China has remained in essence Chinese for three or four thousand years and Japan for half that period. They had a continuing and deep 'reverberating' note.

What that note actually is took me fifteen years to discover in Japan and I am still struggling to understand in China now.

Jaspers had assumed that Japan, being a great literary civilisation which absorbed so much from China, was part of the Axial Age. What I discovered, alongside other others who worked on Japan, particularly S. N. Eisenstadt and Robert Bellah, is that Jaspers too easily assumed this.

Japan over a thousand years rejected Axiality, first from China, which came in several waves and then of the West in several further onslaughts. It has remained, at its core, undivided. It is both soaked in invisible power – everywhere there are temples and little rituals, Shinto and Buddhism are powerful forces. Yet there is simultaneously no seperate, other, world. The dead go nowhere, there is no God, no real heaven. Even to talk of 'Religion' as an instituted field (there is no word for 'religion' in Japanese) is a mistake. Confucianism was partially absorbed, but subverted, and in any case there is a decided absence of interest in another world or parallel forces in Chinese Confucianism, as we have seen.

When I discovered that Japan was basically an ancient, shamanic, civilisation behind the mirror of modern institutions and technology, I put this down to its remote location and its well-honed ability to retain its shamanic integrity against the pressures of outside actualities. I now realise that the early 'vaccination' by Chinese philosophies was made more powerful by being rather mild, namely that the dose Japan received in the seventh to ninth centuries from China and then again in the thirteenth to fifteenth centuries with Buddhism, was rather a mild, half 'Axiality' or in modern parlance, 'Axiality-lite'.

Basically, the mixture of Taoism, Confucianism and Buddhism coming by way of China was very different to the stronger Axiality of India and Persia, and even more different from the full and complete Axiality of Greece and western monotheisms. Axiality is not a black-and-white phenomenon, it is a continuum of 'more or less'. Japan was non-Axial, though Christianity has now infiltrated to tinge its essence.

Japan can at first feel very familiar, a westerner finding his or her own civilisation in the shops and goods, a Chinese finding the colours and temples very similar. Yet this is an illusion. Unless we, and in particular the Chinese, understand this — and the Japanese understand it about themselves in relation to China – relations between these neighbours are likely to remain locked in misunderstanding and mutual recrimination. This account is an attempt to translate between these cultures and to show that what looks at first like brothers or cousins, are indeed strangers, who could be understood and, if respected for their differences, treated as honoured friends.

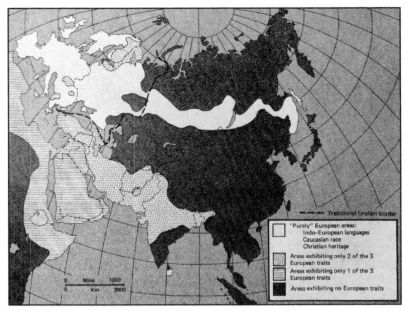

[From Terry G. Jordan, *The European Culture Area (Harper, 1973)*]

The Eurosphere

I STUDIED SOME European history, especially the Napoleonic period, at school, but my first practical encounter with
continental Europe began when I set off in 1959 to hitch-hike
along the route that the young William Wordsworth had taken
a century and a half earlier. The experience of travel through the
years was enriched by various types of reading. At Oxford I took
a paper on European history and when I introduced a 'European
Anthropology' option into the Cambridge Social Anthropology
Tripos, for which I had to read widely. I found that European
sociologists (particularly Montesquieu, Tocqueville, Marx,
Weber, Durkheim and Jaspers), historians (particularly Guizot,

Burkhardt, Marc Bloch and Fernand Braudel), and miscellaneous travellers and writers (particularly Montaigne, Hippolyte Taine, Huizinga), became my favourite authors.

All of these visits, discussions and readings have fed into my idea of continental Europe and given me a sense of the very great difference between different parts of the Continent, as well as the wide gap between all of Europe and the lands to the East (Turkey onwards) and the north (the U.K. and Anglosphere).

I don't recall having any particular assumptions about what I would find on the Continent before I became immersed in various aspects of its present and past, though I must have had them. It all seemed so rich, varied, warm and cultured. I was naturally thrilled at the art, architecture, literature, music, folk culture, while at the same time being saddened at the evidence of constant wars and widespread hardship up to very recently. I was also aware that in Portugal, Spain and Greece, as well as all of Eastern Europe, until well into my adulthood, authoritarian governments still existed.

Yet by the 1980's, Continental Europe seemed to have slipped the shadow of its recent, genocidal and war-mongering past. In the last twenty-seven years, since the fall of the Soviet Union and opening up of Eastern Europe, and the spread of the European Union and other organizations, as well as mass tourism and travel, the surface similarities across this wide area have clearly grown. Yet even my first encounters and travels, let alone a brief reading of the history and sociology of Europe, shows how there are continued deep structural differences between different parts.

To understand these deeper features may be particularly useful for Asian readers, who would easily tend to think that the Eurosphere and the Anglosphere are much the same and to assume that they all bask in general peace, consumerism, rich cultures and a strong Christian tradition.

It is some of these deeper differences, combined with some significant core values and institutional similarities, which I shall try to summarize. It is a difficult task in a few pages when dealing with over a thousand years of a highly diverse and ever-changing continent.

Where and what is Europe?

Where and what is Europe? Let me start with where Europe begins and ends. I remember being surprised when I asked a Japanese friend where he thought the 'West' started and he said in China. When I put the same question to a Chinese friend, he said 'India'. It was clear that he, and others I have spoken to in both Japan and China, see a fundamental difference between the Mongoloid world of East and Southeast Asia, which is Asia proper, and the area stretching from Bengal to Spain which is somehow fundamentally different and can be lumped under the rough heading of 'Indo-European'. I now realize what they mean.

The Japanese and Chinese informants were clearly touching on a real phenomenon. If we take four criteria – language, race, religion, social structure – the whole area from eastern India (though not the Dravidian south of India) through to Portugal or Sweden has three out of four of these.

The vast region is predominantly Caucasian in race. In terms of language, people in the whole of the area, with some small exceptions, speak one or other variant of an Indo-European language. In terms of social structure, the whole is based on the principles of four, occupationally-defined, social orders.

Basically for much of its history all of this area has had four, blood-based, 'castes', with sub-castes within each. There are the Rulers, the *kshatrya* or warriors of India, the nobility of France or Spain, separated off legally and ritually from the lower orders. Often in association with an Emperor or King they are the political rulers. No one could join this blood-based group except by birth.

Then there are the religious orders, the Brahmins in India, ritually the most pure, the mullahs in Islam, the Christian clergy further west. The next order is of the townsmen – the traders and merchants, the 'bourgeois' (*bourge* – town) as the French call them. In India they are again a hereditary and blood-borne caste, the *vaishya*. Finally, at the bottom, reversing the Chinese and Japanese ordering, there are the vast sea of largely illiterate agricultural workers in the villages. Such a fourfold stratification covered all of the area from Calcutta to Lisbon until the later nineteenth century. It still exists over much of this area to this day.

There is a very powerful division throughout this region, between the 'elite culture' of the professional groups, the literate and refined with wide horizons, mostly city dwellers, the 'Great Tradition' of written culture, and the 'Little tradition' or 'popular culture' of the mass of the population. The latter live in a very different, oral, world of myths and rituals largely incomprehensible to those in the elite. This huge division in culture is not to be found in the same shape in our other examples in the Far East or in the Anglosphere.

The final criterion, namely religion, would at first appear to separate this vast area from India to Spain into two blocks. In India, there are the pantheisms (many gods) of the Hindus and the non-God of the Buddhists. Yet even there, there is strong admixture, particularly in east Bengal, Pakistan and north-western India of monotheistic Islam.

The other main block, from the Middle East westwards, is monotheistic, though it is divided into three competing versions, Judaism, Christianity and Islam. These three tradi-tions of monotheism were often at war with each other, nevertheless they share a deep unity with others further to the East, namely that all of the philosophical systems, from the Hindus and Buddhists through to the Zoroastrians and the old Testament prophets and Greek philosophers had gone through that great change which created an autonomous and separated sphere which many call 'Religion'.

Though very different, the traditions, like the alphabetic languages which were universal in this area, as opposed to the pictographic or logographic writings of China and Japan, united the area.

So there is a rough 'family resemblance' over this landscape, people from Calcutta to Rome were 'cousins'. Yet the area is so large, and the differences significant enough, to make it sensible to narrow down our consideration to what would nowadays be termed 'Europe', that is roughly the area which has all four of the characteristics – language, race, monotheistic religion and a four-fold social order. This is the area from the Ural mountains in central Russia through to Scandinavia, from Greece through to Portugal.

One striking feature is the great diversity within a relatively small area. The whole region is smaller than China, both in geography and population, yet its topography, lack of firm borders and turbulent history, has meant that for much of its existence it has been composed of a multitude of states, cultures and traditions with a greater difference from one another than one finds even in China.

Linguistic and geographical diversity

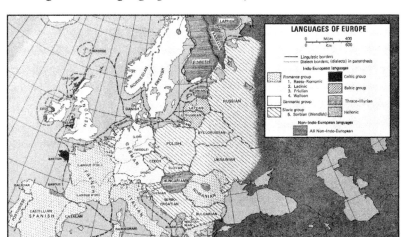

[From Terry G. Jordan, The European Culture Area (Harper, 1973)]

Let me start with language. There was a half millennium when most of the educated could write and speak Latin, and this partly unified western Europe with a common language not dissimilar to the function of Mandarin in China. This unity broke apart half a millenium ago and only recently has English become a common language.

If we move from the top one or two per cent who understood Latin, down from the high culture, the mass of the population spoke a multitude of languages and dialects.There were, of course, the great divisions, between the Romance languages of the Mediterranean up to France, and the Germanic languages of the north and east. The West and East were again split into the Romance and Germanic languages of the west and the eastern languages, including Slavic, Hungarian and Turkic further to the east.

This was just the surface of the linguistic disunity. Only in the later nineteenth century, with the invention of the 'imagined communities' of nation-states, were nations linguistically unified, speaking a common and comprehensible language. Before that the Basques, the Catalans, people who spoke the Langue d'Oc or Langue d'Oil, or Bretons to the north, were just some of the diverse linguistic communities, speaking not just different dialects, but languages. If you travelled a few miles you were often in a different linguistic world. Within each of these separate worlds, there were sharp dialect differences.

The linguistic variations are just one feature of other cultural and social variations over small areas. As Eugene Weber's *Peasants into Frenchmen* (1976) describes, everything could change over ten or twenty miles. The food, housing styles, village shapes, costumes, agricultural instruments, wedding customs, humour, myths and legends varied from small region to small region, as can be seen in some of the great museums of continental Europe.

In terms of the material world, there was a great divide running roughly across the middle of France through into Germany. The agricultural systems of the area of the light, unwheeled, Roman plough suitable for the sandy soils of the south, and the area which used the heavy, wheeled, Germanic plough in northern Europe were very different. It was a contrast, as Marc Bloch described, which led by way of different field and village shapes into different social structures and even personality.

So the land of olives and vines, small villages and fields of the South was structurally different from the wheat and hops and apple area of northern Europe. The south drank wine and ate olives and vegetables as its staples; the north drank beer and cider, and ate bread, cheese and meat.

Religious diversity

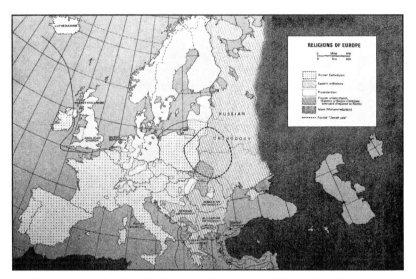

[From Terry G. Jordan, The European Culture Area (Harper, 1973)]

So we come to the huge religious divisions in Europe, splitting the area in a geographical and political way which is largely incomprehensible to many outsiders. The endless wars of religion fought both within Europe and between Europe and its closest neighbouring monotheism, Islam, is a central dynamic of European history. Not content to split into Christians versus Moslems, Christendom split in two Catholic churches, western, Roman, and eastern, Orthodox. And then the western Roman branch split after the sixteenth century into the southern, Roman, and the northern, Protestant.

Religion in one form or another dominated Europe in a way which, if one comes from the world of Taoism or Shinto, of Confucianism and Buddhism, is almost incomprehensible as I have found in discussions with my Chinese and Japanese friends. Religion to their amazement does not seem just to be a matter of ceremonies and small rituals, of social ethics and responsibility. It is so important that it spreads out into all parts of life.

The great European cathedrals and numerous churches, the schools and universities, the literature, the music, the politics and the wars, the language and the philosophical concepts (including those of science), all were soaked in religion.No word, thought or gesture can be made even today amongst those raised in this tradition, even if they think they have long moved away from formal religious beliefs, without in fact indirectly being deeply influenced by this religious heritage.

Europeans carry vestiges of religion in their feelings of guilt, sin, fear of death, attitudes to animals and to pain, artistic appreciation, attitudes to money and saving, attitudes to truth and politics. A Chinese or Japanese visitor is likely to be astonished by this. It is so huge an influence, all around us like the air we breathe, that it can become invisible to the people who are caught up in it, modern Europeans and Americans.

Yet if we want to understand anything in Europe, from the growth of education and science, the Renaissance, Bach or Mozart's music, the invasion of Iraq, the legal and political systems of the West, we have to reckon with monotheistic religion. All aspects of life have a flavour from the widespread influence of Christianity, in the same ways that all of Jewish or Islamic life is filled with God or Allah. One obvious effect of this religious obsession, combined with the constant military contests, can be seen in the nature of the outward imperial expansion of Europe.

A very brief introduction to Christianity

In dealing with the Prophetic revealed religion of Buddhism, I gave a few indications of some of the central tenets. For those in the world, who are not Christians and perhaps know little about it, I will do the same in relation to Christianity. The most succinct way to do this is to give three of the central statements of the faith, which I learnt as a child and when I was confirmed into the Anglican Church.

One of these is shared with Judaism and Islam and supposedly delivered by God to Moses on Mount Sinai many thousands of years ago. There are many translations of this. One of these is:

The Ten Commandments

1. *I am the Lord thy God! Thou shalt have no other Gods but me!*
2. *Thou shalt not take the Name of the Lord thy God in vain!*
3. *Thou shalt keep the Sabbath Day holy!*
4. *Thou shalt honour father and mother!*
5. *Thou shalt not kill!*
6. *Thou shalt not commit adultery!*
7. *Thou shalt not steal!*
8. *Thou shalt not bear false witness against thy neighbor!*
9. *Do not let thyself lust after thy neighbor's wife!*
10. *Thou shalt not covet thy neighbor's house, nor his farm, nor his cattle, nor anything that is his!*

As well as learning these ten commandments, and wondering as a growing boy about the likelihood, and even meaning, of committing adultery, lusting after my neighbour's wife and coveting my neighbour's cattle, I was also taught to say the Lord's Prayer each day. This was supposedly conveyed to his disciples by Jesus and we were taught to say it each night before we went to sleep, and at most of the Christian services we attended.

The traditional version in the translation into English of the bible in the early seventeenth century is as follows.

The Lord's Prayer

Our Father, which art in heaven,
Hallowed be thy Name.
Thy Kingdom come.
Thy will be done in earth,
As it is in heaven.
Give us this day our daily bread.
And forgive us our trespasses,
As we forgive them that trespass against us.
And lead us not into temptation,
But deliver us from evil.
For thine is the kingdom,
The power, and the glory,
For ever and ever.
Amen.

The third key text, the affirmation of faith or Apostles' Creed which we had to learn by heart when we were confirmed into the Anglican Communion, usually around puberty, is as follows (in a 1988 translation).

The Creed

I believe in God, the Father almighty,
creator of heaven and earth.
I believe in Jesus Christ, God's only Son, our Lord,
who was conceived by the Holy Spirit,
born of the Virgin Mary,
suffered under Pontius Pilate,
was crucified, died, and was buried;
he descended to the dead.
On the third day he rose again;
he ascended into heaven,
he is seated at the right hand of the Father,

and he will come to judge the living and the dead.
I believe in the Holy Spirit,
the holy catholic Church,
the communion of saints,
the forgiveness of sins,
the resurrection of the body,
and the life everlasting. Amen.

In these three core statements, which we memorized, we have many of the central tenets of Christianity: the belief in one almighty, merciful, creator God; the birth of his Son who was crucified, died and arose from the dead; the resurrection of our bodies and life everlasting. It was a strongly ethical religion, founded on the mystery of the Trinity (God, Son and Holy Ghost).

Missionary expansion and nationalism

The earliest Imperial adventures of Alexander and the Romans had been for conquest and booty. Yet from the discovery of America through to the Vietnam war, the 'blood dimmed tide', as W. B. Yeats might have put it, of Western con-tinental imperialism – the Portuguese, Spanish, Italian, French and Belgian in particular, was based on the dual purpose of ransacking (booty) and Christianity. Spreading God's word with fire and sword, settling new land by the extermination or enslavement of the indigenous populations and the forcible conversion to Christianity, this was the constant theme.

Given this aggressive outward thrust, a mixture of gunpowder weapons and the Bible, it is not surprising that by the time the tide had started to lap on the Japanese and Chinese coasts in the sixteenth century, those peoples became wary.

The religions of the East are not evangelical – people are not met at the door by Taoists or Confucians trying to sell them their religion. They are not told that they will go to hell unless they find the true faith. Yet this was what the Crusades onwards had been in the West. People were to be crucified, burnt alive, tortured and imprisoned if they did not accept your variant of the truth.

Added to this was another feature which is not found in China, but any Chinese now needs to understand, and that is nationalism. One of the problems facing all these small, scarcely defined, groups of people living in the outcrops of the Western rim of the Eurasian continent, whether Spain, Italy, France or Germany, was how to unite populations who spoke many languages and did not naturally feel 'French' or 'Spanish' or 'Italian'.

One way to do this, and a necessity in a sea of mistrust and highly armed neighbours, was through emphasizing what is often called the 'ideal' or 'imagined' community. Such a community is a subgroup who can be persuaded that they have a shared history, blood, culture and political system and which can make people die for their country and obey their rulers, and speak of themselves as 'We the French'.

Such national sentiments, uniting a few million or more, had in fact probably existed long before the 'print-capitalism' which is supposed to have made it possible from the eighteenth century onwards. We find it much earlier in small, bounded, places like England, Portugal or Sweden. Yet Benedict Anderson is right in arguing that continental European nations are largely a nineteenth and twentieth century invention.

The world imagined by nationalism sees an underlying undivided landscape split into 'natural' borders which divide us from our enemies. The tragic history of over two centuries of recent warfare, from the Napoleonic wars through two World Wars, where almost identical peoples, supposedly practicing a common, loving, religion, tore each other to pieces, and in the process exported their tensions to the Far East and involved China and Japan in a titanic struggle, is well-known. Combined with ever-improving gunpowder weaponry, it made western history one long battle, where 'ignorant armies clash by night', torn apart and then regrouping.

Confrontation and law

It is not absolutely clear how this warlike history of small proto-nations fighting each other, plus the linguistic and religious divisions, are related to a fundamental difference between East Asia and Indo-Europe. Yet a Chinese visitor will be struck by the basic difference between the ideal of a consensual, harmonious, civilisation in China and the open ideal of confrontational, aggressive, argumentative, tension which is characteristic of European civilisation.

One area where we can see this in practice is in the law. Europeans are not only 'religion soaked', but also 'litigation soaked'. The dialectical, confrontational, pursuit of truth and knowledge we find in Greek philosophy, may have been one of the factors which lies behind one of the most developed aspects of Roman civilisation – the law codes. These were also clearly influenced by the legal emphasis in Judaism and Christianity and formed into an intricate legal code, set into a strong form in the late Roman Empire under Justinian, This tradition has shaped Europe to this day. These Roman codes, like other aspects of Roman and Greek civilisation, were reinvigorated in the fifteenth and sixteenth centuries and spread across all of the lands of Continental Europe.

Several significant features of these powerful legal codes which would interest an Asian visitor are worth noting. One is that they were hierarchical – they put huge and absolute power in the hands of the ruler, the Emperor or King, who had a divine right to rule which could not, unlike the Chinese Emperor under the 'Mandate of Heaven', be contested.

This absolutist tendency, derived from late imperial Rome, was one of the reasons why the revived codes were so strongly supported by the European monarchies in Spain, France and the Holy Roman Empire from the fifteenth century onwards. This revived Roman Law was the foundation of the absolutisms of Europe and Russia in the eighteenth century. A continuation of this tradition seems likely to be one of the factors behind the Fascism which conquered all of the European continental world in the middle of the twentieth century, holding almost all of the old Roman Empire from Spain to Germany in its grip.

The second feature was that all laws were based on birth status. Roman law endorses slavery, differentiates the humbly born from the nobly born, recognise the father as innately superior to the child and the man as innately superior to the woman. In some ways it was like Confucianism, yet magnified through instituted laws rather than education.

Thirdly Roman Law had a particular view of property. The concepts of a 'bundle of rights' in property, of the possibility of absolute private property, of the sanctity of property against all powers, which we find in English Common Law, was absent. The great German lawyers could not understand what the English really meant by Trusts, by Equity, and by the confusions and intricacies of their property laws.

The Roman Law division between things and people was absolute. The artificial corporations, the possibility of disinheritances through a will, the complex arrangements of the English banking systems, all this was a mystery. Hence, as Max Weber noted, it was not out of Roman Law but Common Law that the instruments of market capitalism were developed.

Finally there is the matter of criminal legal process. The

legal system was totally integrated into the political system in Roman Law. There was no separation of law and politics. Law was a tool of government. The law was not there to protect the citizen, but to further the controlling functions of the state. It was the world which lay behind Michel Foucault's *Discipline and Punish* (1975), behind the Inquisition and the pact with the church, behind the judicial use of torture and the simplified process whereby the investigating forces, the police, and the judge and prosecutor were often the same person.

There were no balances or protections for the subject; no juries, no 'habeas corpus' (right to know what one was accused of and release unless a charge was quickly made), no assumption of innocence until one was proven guilty, no right to defence lawyers, no necessity for a set of strong and direct proofs. In the Continental Roman system, the examining magistrate arrested a person and tried to find people who would incriminate him or her, often under the threat or use of torture, and often with the utmost secrecy. It is no wonder that the vast mass of the illiterate peasantry, kept in order by an armed *gendarmerie* and subject to brutal trials and torture, hated the state and its obvious lackeys.

The European legal system has now absorbed some of the Anglo-American based on the power of contract, equity and human rights, the 'Rule of Law' and due process. Yet it is worth remembering this long legacy before we in the West congratulate ourselves on our love of human rights and the rule of law and urge them with zeal on other traditions.

The limits of growth in Europe

Ever since the Enlightenment speculations of Montesquieu and Adam Smith, one of the central questions has been 'what happened to block China'. There is a widespread consensus that by the Southern Song period in the 13th century, China had the most advanced technology, the greatest economy, the most peaceful, rich and knowledgeable civilisation on Earth. Then China seemed to hit a 'high-level equilibrium trap'. The inspiration subsided, so that, by 1800, half a millenium later, China had not improved or developed much. In particular, the absence of any Renaissance or Scientific Revolution, or start of an Industrial Revolution, can seem puzzling. Yet, if we turn the mirror round and look from China, we can ask almost exactly the same question about Europe. 'Why did Europe become "stuck", lose its way, start to slide backwards, from the seventeenth century onwards?'

Looking at Europe in the twelfth to sixteenth centuries, we are impressed by its immense energy; filled with bustling cities, free republics, a rapidly improving agriculture and mining technology. It was expanding outwards with its Empires and trade to encompass the globe. It had fine universities, was importing Arabic and Ancient Greek science, producing beautiful art. Despite the huge setback of the Black Death in the fourteenth century, Europe seemed destined to progress beyond the limits of an agrarian society and to move into something new and magnificent.

Much of this dynamic energy, creativity and openness arose from the balance of powers which emerged after the fall of the Roman Empire. Francois Guizot's *History of Europe* (1828) explained how, building on some of the earlier knowledge and technology of the Greeks and Romans, a new civilisation was born in the period between the eighth and twelfth centuries. This flourished because the forces which lie at the basis of a civilisation were all roughly balanced and no single one could gain a stranglehold.

The royal power was kept in check by an alliance of the nobility and the cities; the clergy and the lawyers often formed an alliance with the King, but sometimes opposed him. The peasantry benefited from this tension and division and were thriving, with new ploughs and the wider use of water and wind power, new crops and greater freedom from taxation.

Thus, anyone looking at Europe in around 1600, visiting Venice or Madrid, Florence or Amsterdam, would have predicted some kind of continued economic, cultural and intellectual growth in the independent universities, popular assemblies, courts with their rich and discerning patrons. It all looked so hopeful. Yet only a century and a half later much of Europe had declined and misery was increasing for many.

Economic growth, as Adam Smith noted, had stopped and formerly rich nations like Spain and Italy were declining, their peasantries immiserated, their nobility increasingly impoverished. Even the great merchant centres of Venice and Amsterdam had peaked and started to decline.

It is clear that from the late sixteenth century through to the middle of the nineteenth century the mass of the peasantry in Europe were having to work harder, had less animal power at their disposal, were more highly taxed.

Even the Dutch Republic, according to Smith the wealthiest part of Europe per capita, was stagnant by the early eighteenth century and by the end of that century so weak that it was easily conquered by Napoleon and had to be shored up (literally) with British aid of two million pounds in order to stop it becoming flooded.

The stasis or decline was also true in the world of ideas. The great universities of Spain, Italy and France were largely empty shells by the mid-eighteenth century and were closed by Napoleon, before being re-instituted as government-controlled, administrative training centres, in the nineteenth century. The seeking after new knowledge of the age of Copernicus and Galileo had waned by the end of the seventeenth century. There was little experimental science of any worth being done over much of the continent.

The artistic glories of the period of the Italian, Dutch and Spanish Renaissance petered out in the seventeenth century. Though music in Germany, and philosophy and literature in France, continued at a high level, there was definitely a general slowing down.

Behind all this was a loss of the balance of powers. The republics were closing down, Royal power was increasing as it formed a stronger alliance with the religious orders, supported by absolutist Roman law which spread across Europe, giving Kings and Emperors new and divine rights.

So when the Baron de Montesquieu published his *Persian Letters* (1721) and *Spirit of the Laws* (1748) he had to do so in Switzerland, away from the Inquisition and censorship of the State which would have crushed the books in France. As well as France and Germany, in Russia with Peter the Great and Catherine the Great, and elsewhere in the Holy Roman Empire, powerful States dominated the West.

So we can see that in the two hundred years from around 1600, Europe tended to become poorer, more despotic and less creative. It was going backwards, or at the best static – still subject to periodic and devastating famines, still engaged in huge internal wars, still trying to squeeze money from the rest of the world through slavery and colonialism.

In the light of all this, as Smith observed, China was both normal and in many ways superior. As he observed, China was not retreating, it was still full of busy cities and active agriculture. If it was not markedly improving since the Song, at least it was doing pretty well.

Comparing these two ends of Eurasia, we can see that both areas had hit a ceiling which Smith analyzed carefully. He saw the stasis as inevitable, an obvious limit in a world where almost all energy still came from the sun through animals and plants. This was a world where, in Edward Gibbon's view in the later eighteenth century , three quarters of mankind (which at that time meant about 560 out of the 750 million humans) lived in misery and poverty.

If we skip forward to the later nineteenth century, the period of nationalism, industrialisation, the use of chemistry in agriculture, new energy from coal, we may easily believe that at last Europe had escaped by a miracle from the high-level trap. In some ways it had, certainly in terms of knowledge and material wealth. Yet the political traps remained.

It is perhaps not too far-fetched to believe that the curious lurching to the extremes of left and right, Communism in Russia, Fascism all over central and western Europe in the 1930s, was somehow related to the earlier buffers.

What had happened with Roman law and absolutist government was that all of civil society, the balancing, countervailing, forces had been undermined and absorbed until all was in the hands of a government that, within its means, attempted to be absolutist. It was, like the Chinese Emperor, dependent on its administrative assistants, and they in turn were entirely dependent on royal patronage. The universities, the churches, the cities, the courts, the armed forces, all were increasingly weakened and subservient.

This pattern was spread in a few years by Hitler, Stalin, Mussolini and Franco. 'Fascism' is a word (*fascisti*) which refers to the bundling together of powers into an indivisible mass, the joining of the economy, polity, ideology and society. The fascists dismantled the remaining traces of that three quarters of a millennium, from the end of Rome to the Renaissance, which Guizot had documented, that division of powers and growth of a rich and plural civil society.

If we understand this, we are reminded that in one sense,

the divergence of China and Europe was not as great as some might think. Until the 1850s both were facing the structural problems of creating a living before the age of fossil fuels and the knowledge of chemistry and medicine which would suddenly relieve much of the burden.

Landward and seaward civilisations

Yet while there were deeper, very similar, structural problems as between Europe and China, there were also immense differences in the resources available for their solution. One of the striking facts about China is that if we think of it as a vast four-sided box, three of the sides are land borders and most of its people live many days away from the sea. In China there are immense rivers, waterways and lakes, but the lure of longer distance trade along the coasts and out to sea is less compelling. China looks towards the Silk Roads and South East Asia. It had in the fourteenth century discovered Africa and perhaps America, but not pursued this discovery.

Western Europe, like Japan, is bounded by seas – the Baltic, Atlantic, Mediterranean and the Black Sea. Although the huge inland plains of central Europe are different, the majority of people living in the much smaller countries of Europe were within a few hours or days of the sea.

It has often been observed that seaports are homes to freedom, both of political independence and intellectual freedom, from Venice, through Lisbon and Montesquieu's Bordeaux, up to Adam Smith's Glasgow and David Hume's Edinburgh. Wide and deep thinking, the clash and inflow of new ideas brought in on the sea, a cosmopolitan liberal world seems to flourish in these cities.

Furthermore, looking outwards from the Italian, Spanish or French seaports people had a growing interest in long-distance trade, and soon a rush of new foods and drinks and the shock of new customs and wealth began to be absorbed. The constant flow of new things and experiences help to stimulate people, to surprise and energize them, and of course provided huge wealth.

China by the Song dynasty was largely complete in its culture, though it would expand geographically in the Qing. When it closed off long-distance trading towards India and beyond in the Ming dynasty, this inflow of new knowledge, things and wealth partly dried up, except with trading partners in its satellites and Southeast Asia and along the silk roads. Europe was bounded but very leaky, China mainly bounded.

An urban civilisation

As we have seen with law, one very marked feature of continental Western Europe was the impact of the Roman Empire. Although it had collapsed, many of the institutions and features of the late Empire were either absorbed by the waves of Germanic peoples who conquered it, or revived later.

So the roads, waterways, machinery, late Roman religion, city shapes, were all gradually re-installed alongside Roman law through the Middle Ages. Much of Europe became a new, Roman-flavoured, Holy Roman Empire. Two particular features of this continuity remind me a little of the way in which China absorbed the barbarian waves of Mongols and Manchus and turned them into Han Chinese.

One of these is that Rome was an urban civilisation. Centred on the great cities of Rome and Alexandria, the characteristic was that 'civilisation' and 'civility', coming from the Roman word for city, were synonymous with the city. The literate, powerful and wealthy tended to live in the cities and the city walls were the boundary between 'culture' and 'nature', the 'High' and the 'Low'. The fully human elite, and the rabble of slaves and peasants, were divided between town and country.

This urban-based philosophy continues to this day. The city is where the thinkers, artists, top professionals and rulers live, even if they have the occasional palace or holiday home in selected country spots. If there is a need to scatter a powerful nobility elsewhere, they live in large, fortified, châteaus, which dominate the nearby town appended to them.

The city is the abode of a thriving and, as one moves northwards through Europe, increasingly independent merchant and artistic community, a rich and educated bourgeoisie as in Paris, Antwerp or Amsterdam. All this, as we have noted, is very different from China where the cities were just denser versions of the countryside with some Mandarins and some Imperial troops – fortresses with large markets.

Family systems

One great division in Europe, suggested by John Hajnal, is between the family systems, particularly the age at first marriage and the degree to which marriage is universal. Those who lived west of a line drawn from Trieste in north western Italy to St Petersburg (Leningrad) in Russia, exhibit the West European pattern, and those to the east of that line another system. Those to the west married late (in their mid-twenties) and selectively (up to a quarter of women never marrying), those to the east married in their teens and almost all women married.

Other aspects of the family system were also very different between the Mediterranean south, where there were often more intense relations between parents and children, and the more fragmented systems of northern Europe.

Although there were profound differences within Europe, it is also worth noting two outstanding similarities, and also differences, between Europe and China in terms of the articulation between family, state and society. On the one hand, since one's blood ancestry was traced through both males and females in Europe there were, except in small pockets (for example in the Balkans), no clans of the Chinese kind. There were no ancestor halls, no clan villages, no very strong, named, blood groupings.

So, in many ways, unlike China, the continental Europeans could not place kinship as their basic infrastructure or organising principle. Kinship dominated much of Chinese life, determining marriage, job prospects, political allegiances, access to ancestral blessings. There is not nearly as much emphasis on this in Europe, though there were times and places, for example in the Mafia areas of southern Italy and Sicily, or the blood vendettas of the Balkans or the Scottish Highlands up to 1745, where there is something of the Chinese flavour of intense blood bonds.

So there is a great difference between Europe and china in the structure and meaning of the family. In Europe, the power of the family was limited by the countervailing forces of a strong religion, advanced economy and towns, powerful feudal lords and rulers. On the other hand, if we look at the family systems of China and Europe from Japan or the Anglosphere, we notice a strong resemblance between them in certain respects, which make both of those continents very different from the two island cases.

In Europe and China, the father's power is very great and the birth family remains the basis of social life. We can see this most easily in the legal systems of Europe and China. Until recently, the legal systems of Europe and China gave extreme power to the parents, balanced by a life right in family property to the children. Parents had patriarchal power and were due a lifelong respect and support. Children might move away physically, but never psychologically, from their parents.

This is very different from the situation in Japan and the Anglosphere.

Education

The machine for generating the split between the social and economic, the destruction of the ultimate 'atom of kinship' which we will investigate more fully in the Anglosphere, is the educational system. In France and even in Dutch and Belgian schools, education is seen as a place for mental training and some ethical advice. The school is not a place which takes you out of the family into wider society. It is not a device for setting a person 'free', politically, socially, economically and religiously, from their parents.

In this respect the Confucian system, which did not in any way threaten the power of the absolute father, was similar. Education was a tool for family advancement, training in skills which the family could not provide. This means that throughout Continental Europe children are still left largely under the influence of their close family, especially parents and siblings. They never become fully independent, even when they marry.

If we regard full individualistic 'modernity' as a state where the spheres of economy, society, politics and religion are finally separated and an individual is 'free' to act as he or she wishes without being deeply controlled by the family, then Bruno Latour was right (but only about the European system) when he wrote a book titled *We Have Never Been Modern* (1993).

Continental Europeans still live in a partly embedded world, for good (warmth, meaning, support) and evil (conformist, only partially free). They live in a world where 'corruption' (nepotism, Mafia, the mixing of family and other spheres of life) is more likely, especially as much of life is a war against the threatening State.

They live in a world of hierarchy, God, Jesus, Mary and the patron saints. The religious patrons are aligned with the family pattern. They live in a world, as Tocqueville noted, of occupational castes, where many middle-class families perpetuate their positions as lawyers, merchants, teachers or doctors through the centuries. They live in a world where the elite educational channels are not open to all.

The expression of a much more familistic feel to the continental peoples often strikes outsiders. Many continental families, as in China, express their family warmth through large communal meals and an enormous importance in sharing food and drink. A strong distinction between 'we' the family, who are entertained and trusted, and 'they' strangers or even colleagues, who are not trusted or felt to be close, has been sensed by many from outside.

'Amoral familism' (behaving as if moral life is confined to the family) is an extreme form, as Edward Banfield points out in southern Europe, and the world of 'honour and shame' centering on the Mediterranean with its male chauvinism and protection of women's virginity, is another facet. Hints of this strong familistic feeling, familiar to a Highland Scot or southern Irishman, is different from much of the Anglosphere experience as we shall see.

A structural civilisation

China is understandable as a 'structural' civilisation. It is based on the relations between people and between things – black and white, men and women, Yin and Yang. All meaning, as in Japan, lies in the *relation* and not in the *thing*.

Again, though it is not as extreme, there is a family resemblance here to Indo-European civilisation. It has long been established that India can be regarded as a structural civilisation, based on the oppositions and relations of castes, genders, the pure and the impure. From early days in France, up to modern structuralists like Claude Lévi-Strauss, Roland Barthes and Michel Foucault, there is a way of thinking in terms which feel very different from the Anglosphere tradition of thinkers like Hobbes, Locke or even of Germans like Max Weber.

The gendered oppositions of Romance languages, male and female, superior and inferior, the structured, status-based, social systems in law, even perhaps the philosophy of Descartes, strike me as very different from the stolidly empirical, individualist, Anglosphere world that I have been brought up in.

If one were to put all this on a continuum, then Japan is completely structuralist; China, so well understood by French structuralists, is strongly structuralist but not completely. Europe combined structuralism with other modes into a balance, while the Anglosphere is almost purely individualist and non-structuralist.

Cultural magnificence

This brief overview of Europe, seems to present at times a rather negative picture. There are reasons for this. There is room for some counter to Euro-centric arrogance. There is also a strong sense of early promise giving way to later disappointment. There is the terrible tragedy of constant wars, famines and diseases within Europe. There is the appalling record of European imperialism and destruction of many beautiful worlds. There is the intolerance, persecution, slavery and political absolutism. There are indeed many negative features.

Yet it is worth giving some counterbalance to the above, a corrective to the sense of disappointment which may also arise from Europe's current anxieties and uncertainties in the face of disunity, migration and relative economic stagnation. It is wrong to bury Europe's achievements too quickly, for they are in many ways absolutely extraordinary.

Whatever field of human endeavour we examine over the last thousand years we find that Europe made an amazing contribution. Travelling from Spain to Italy, France to Germany, and through eastern and northern Europe, we are struck by the physical remains of outstanding beauty, in architecture, sculpture and painting. There can be little doubt that from Giotto through Leonardo da Vinci to Picasso, Europe produced the greatest painting of any world civilisation.

There can be no question that from Monteverdi, through Bach and Mozart up to the 20th century almost all of the world's great classical music emanated from Europe. It is incontestable that almost all of the grandest philosophy and social science, from Montesquieu to Max Weber, and many before and after them, came from Europe. Likewise most of the greatest scientists from Copernicus to Einstein were, of course, European.

In almost every branch of human activity both in heroic, remembered, individuals, in great movements which turned the world on its axis, in particular the Renaissance and Scientific Revolution, to the work of millions of unremembered individuals who built the magnificent cathedrals, castles, palaces, roads and gardens, Europe is arguably the greatest artistic and intellectual centre the world has ever known.

Europe became an interactive network or system over the period of growing wealth from about the tenth century onwards. It was a laboratory for innovative experiments. It was able to absorb first the great legacy of Islam, which had preserved and developed ancient and oriental thought. It could also absorb over time the extraordinary inventions of

Asia and in particular China. Being a sea-surrounded civilisation helped it to import many ideas and materials from the discoveries of new worlds from the fifteenth century onwards.

In every sphere there was a survival of the fittest; the best philosophies, artistic breakthroughs, scientific thought, new technologies of peace and war. So it remained dynamic and by the sixteenth century was evolving into an open new world of exploration at every level.

Even though, as I have suggested, it lost some of its balance and creativity in later centuries, its legacy lives on not only in Europe but in every part of the world. The fashions and technologies of Japan and China, as much as those of England and America, largely stem from this European world. A walk through the great shopping malls of China today shows that they are almost entirely dominated by great continental chains of fashion goods, while outside are parked the German cars.

Certainly without the creativity and dynamism of Europe, there would be no Anglosphere. For although I will treat Britain and the cultures which it influenced as if they were semi-isolated, it is as well to remember that almost all that they created was ultimately derived, certainly before the 18th century, from European models.

It is equally well to remember that Europe was to a large extent the product of ideas and technologies from far outside its bounds, coming along the land and sea silk roads that have bound the world together into one integrated system for thousands of years.

I have found, looking over my own life and experiences, that though I was taught to be 'British', my travels through Europe, Nepal, India, Japan and China constantly reminded me of how this 'Britishness' is a bundle of contradictory imports from all over the world.

Conflicting points of origin

There has always been a potential tension within European history because of the fact that in many ways, unlike all the other civilisations, Europe really has *two* points of origin not one. The earlier point of origin was the more than thousand years of Graeco- Roman civilisation which laid the foundation for later developments. Yet this first foundational point of origin was shattered and mixed up with an entirely different source, that is in the nomadic Germanic warring tribes which brought down the Roman Empire and later the waves of Slavic and Mongolian peoples.

The great civilisation of Rome (absorbing Greek ideas) had covered much of the area which many people consider to be Europe. Yet, after its collapse the roads, viaducts, cities and farms decayed. The legal and political systems of late Rome appeared to wither, even the languages were replaced and new customs and technologies took over. Yet that point of origin was not entirely lost to the forces from the Germanic forests.

So Europe has tended to oscillate between two poles or points of origin. There is authoritarian unity, as in Imperial Rome for several centuries, then the absolutist age centred on the eighteenth century and then the twentieth century between 1917 and 1945. Alternately there is a hugely diverse, multilingual, competitive, free and creative Europe which stemmed from the waves of Germanic and other invasions. Combined together, they have given us most of the greatest music, painting, philosophy and food which we enjoy.

The wider Eurosphere

Although Huntington treats South and Middle America as a separate civilisation, I think it makes more sense to think of them, as we shall do with the wider Anglosphere, as an extension of continental Europe and the Eurosphere. This would also apply, to a lesser degree, to the other parts of the former European colonial empires in Africa, South East Asia and elsewhere. Yet for the moment I shall confine myself to the Hispanic parts of South and Central America.

In most of southern and central America, if we apply the four criteria for 'Europe', that is race, language, religion and social structure, the majority of the people are basically 'European'.

In terms of race, the original destruction of the Aztec and Inca Empires and of most of the other indigenous peoples, where more than three quarters of the original inhabitants were killed by war, famine and disease, it is the incoming Hispanic race which predominates. Thus the predominant racial mix is Caucasoid, though, of course, there is a large mixed or *mestizo,* population combining the Caucasoid settlers with native Amerindian populations, and, later there is a large influx of Africans, originally slaves.

In terms of language, the majority languages are Spanish and Portuguese, though again there are pockets of the Amerindian languages, and mixed creole languages, with some pockets of German, English and the languages of other colonial powers.

In terms of religion, again the dominant one is Christian, of the Roman Catholic branch, spread with the aid of the In-quisition, and a central part of the culture of much of the continent. Again it is mixed with traces of original Amerindi-an beliefs, and also traditions from Africa (voodoo and others) and also, increasingly, Pentecostal Protestant Christian sects.

Finally, in terms of social stratification and law, the central status-based law spread. It recognised the superiority of men over women, of noble blood over common blood, of whites over people of other colours. So it is, in the broad sense in which Tocqueville uses the word to describe birth-given differences, a 'caste' society. There was traditionally a small educated elite surrounded by a huge peasantry. The oppositions of the 'Great' and the 'Little' traditions, of the high and the popular culture which we find across Europe was also present.

Many of the other cultural and structural features overlapped with continental Europe and particularly the Iberian Peninsula and consequently we find much of Spanish and Portuguese culture. The urban bias, the formal, centralised, bureaucracy, the aesthetic styles, the humour and the *machismo* opposition of male and female, have all been deeply influenced by the Continental models which I have outlined above.

I am aware that my treatment of the Eurosphere is somewhat unbalanced because it devotes most of its attention to Western Europe, that is basically to the half of Europe which from 1945 to 1991 was divided by the Iron Curtain. As Norman Davis shows at great length in his massive *Europe: A History* (2010), the proper way to look at Europe is to consider it stretching at least as far as the Ural Mountains in central Russia. Indeed, in the map of Europe according to the four criteria, it can be seen that it stretches much further than that across to eastern Russia and the borders of China.

My own Western-centric vision is caused by many of the things which Davis describes – particularly the Cold War division and the way in which we were taught about 'Europe' at school and university. It also reflects the pattern of my own travelling through the continent. Most of my travel has been in the western part until quite recently, when I have been able to visit Poland, Hungary, Czechoslovakia and Slovenia but never Russia or the Baltic states or Ukraine. I have had no first-hand contact with Slavic, Turkic or Hungarian languages or Eastern or Russian Orthodox Christianity.

So my own bias reflects the very real fault-lines which led

Huntington to concentrate on the differences between East and West, and to treat what he called 'Orthodox Civilisation' as a separate case from 'The West'.

Beyond acknowledging the central, deep, unity of all of the western tip of Eur-Asia over many thousands of years, recently examined by Peter Frankopan in *The Silk Roads* (2015) where Frankopan places himself in Eastern Europe and Central Asia as his vantage point, to look east west and south, I cannot really do more.

Obviously, the family systems, forms of language, economies, political systems, forms of Christianity, and mixtures of Islam, makes the East and the West of Europe different in many respects within a wider shared tradition. So we are left in the uncomfortable position that we cannot, I think, follow Huntington in making the Orthodox a separate civilisation, yet we cannot entirely be easy in amalgamating it with central and western Europe.

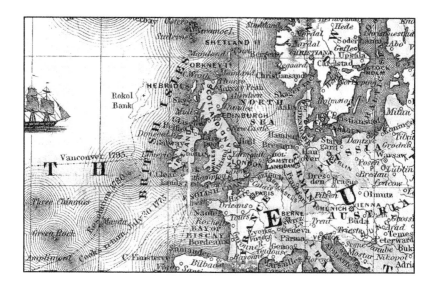

The Anglosphere

LIKE MANY OF my ancestors, including my parents and grandparents, having been born abroad in a remote part of the British Empire (Assam), I was sent 'home' to Britain at an early age (five) to learn to be a member of the Anglosphere. I was to learn something of the history, customs and culture of the British so that my identity would be secure. If the Empire had not collapsed while I was at school, I would perhaps have repeated the pattern of 'migration and return' with my own children.

The twenty years from my return to England until I left Oxford with a doctorate at the age of twenty-five and married, was a kind of 'participant-observation' fieldwork, learning to understand my home society. Explicitly in my lessons in history, literature, art and language, and more implicitly through the games, hobbies, friendships, dormitory, study and house organization of my boarding schools, I learnt the necessary skills and deep habitus that would make me effective in the wider Anglosphere world.

By the end of the process, what had been artificial and needing to be learnt through formal and informal training, had become, like riding a bicycle or swimming, so internalized, so natural, that I would not even be aware of it. I would end up thinking my own civilisation normal and not needing justification, while all other ones, starting with the European Continent and extending to the rest of the world, were different, perhaps slightly odd, perhaps a little less excellent than my own.

From within, it is almost impossible to make the familiar sufficiently unfamiliar that we can understand it at more than an intuitive level. As R. H. Tawney once observed, 'He little of England knows who only England knows'. This is a problem which is particularly great because wherever I go now, the effects of the Anglosphere are to be found, so that what I take for granted is also assumed by others.

What is the Anglosphere?

In his categorization of civilisations, Samuel Huntington has lumped all of western Europe and the former British Empire as 'Western', and for many people in the world this seems intuitively correct. Yet as I came to investigate Britain, and then visited the United States and Australia, and considered the features of the different parts of the ex-European imperial territories, I realized that it is more helpful to split 'The West' into the British area and the places it created, the Anglosphere, and the Eurosphere, with its imperial legacy, particularly in Latin America and parts of Africa and South East Asia.

My unformed feelings about the huge difference were given shape by the book by Claudio Veliz, *The New World of the Gothic Fox* (1994), which outlined the differences between central and southern America, and the English-founded north. This idea was further refined through reading James C. Bennett, *The Anglosphere Challenge* (2004), further developed by Bennett with Michael Lotus in *America 3.0* (2013).

Since the concept may be unfamiliar to many, here is how Bennett described the Anglosphere at the start of his 'An Anglosphere Primer' in 2001.

This term, which can be defined briefly as the set of English-speaking, Common Law nations, implies far more than merely the sum of all persons who employ English as a first or second language. To be part of the Anglosphere requires adherence to the fundamental customs and values that form the core of English- speaking cultures. These include individualism, rule of law, honouring contracts and covenants, and the elevation of freedom to the first rank of political and cultural values.

Nations comprising the Anglosphere share a common historical narrative in which the Magna Carta, the English and American Bills of Rights, and such Common Law principles as trial by jury, presumption of innocence, "a man's home is his castle", and "a man's word is his bond" are taken for granted. Thus persons or communities who happen to communicate or do business in English are not necessarily part of the Anglosphere, unless their cultural values have also been shaped by those values of the historical English-speaking civilisation.

When the Qianlong Emperor in 1793 dismissed the British Embassy of Lord George Macartney as insignificant, he could be forgiven for thinking that the country which had sent the mission was just a tiny, far away, island. It seemed a smaller and somewhat less impressive version of the European powers who for several centuries had been sending traders and missionaries to the celestial court. Little could Qianlong have guessed that, half a century later, that small country would defeat China in two wars and impose humiliating conditions on her.

The natural assumption that the British were really no different from the European continent is as mistaken as the assumption that China and Japan are roughly the same. We have seen that, under a cloak of cultural similarity, Japan developed, like some latter-day Galapagos Islands, flora and fauna almost entirely different from China.

The bounded and separated Japanese islands incubated and retained another world in almost all respects different from its great continental neighbour China. Many people do not realise that the same has happened on an island at the other end of the Eurasian landmass, namely Britain.

I shall document these differences briefly and explain how, even though the English Channel was narrower than the Sea of Japan, Britain developed another world, in many respects different from its continental neighbours, yet concealed under a cloak of a shared Christian heritage, Caucasoid race and Indo-European language.

The peculiar development of Britain, and particularly England, matters more than it might have done if it had been restricted to a small island of a few million people off the western tip of Eur-Asia. This is because Britain developed a package of institutions and structures which are in many ways synonymous with 'modernity', that is market capitalism, industrialism, science, democracy, the rule of law and an open social structure.

These developments became magnified by two events which were linked to their presence. The first was the rapid expansion of this system to cover roughly a quarter of the world's land mass and population in the largest empire in world history – the British Empire. Australia, Canada, India, Burma and many other areas were coloured pink on the maps and are still shaped by the peculiarities of Britain. Many of them decided, after independence, to remain members of the British Commonwealth, historically a very unusual choice. The second was the influence of the Anglosphere-founded former colony, later to become the United States of America.

North America and the Anglosphere

America, as Tocqueville described it in the early nineteenth century, was easy to understand. Having destroyed the indigenous peoples of America, it had no real history. It was built with a blueprint laid out by the Enlightenment thinkers, John Locke and Montesquieu by way of Jefferson and others. This blueprint, encapsulated in the Declaration of Independence and of the Rights of Man and in the Constitution, enshrined the central principles of what had been incubated in England over the centuries.

There was the concept of innate rights of all subjects and citizens – 'Life, Liberty, and the Pursuit of Happiness'. There was also the protection of the individual and the pursuit of wealth through the English Common Law system which was imported largely unchanged into America. There was the power of (richer, male and white) people represented through their delegates in Parliament. There was the separation of religion and politics. There was the devout Christian ideology, shipped with the Puritan fathers. Protestantism was a faith that was viewed as a private matter and should not be directly incorporated into the state.In essence, what America was trying to do was to pin down the quintessence of modernity, that is the formal and explicit separation of politics, economics, ideology and society.

The mechanism for ensuring that each individual lived in such a separated world was the educational system. This separated a child, at least in terms of his or her rights, and was taken to America. Tocqueville noticed how very precocious and independent, confident and rational, were the young people of America when compared to the familistic, immature, dependent, French children he had left behind. So the law, the language, the basic political system, the financial system, some of the games and humour, the family system and the high social mobility and absence of caste were all taken to America from Britain.

All this was magnified and made more extreme because the system was new and lacked some of the encrustaceans and inherited balances of its original. It was

more individualistic, more competitive, more intense and more concerned with making money and becoming a financial success. In particular the United States dropped the monarchy, the separation of Crown and Parliament, turning the President into the ceremonial, the political and the military leader. It abandoned a good deal of the social distinctions of the highly stratified English class system.

Everyone was born free and equal – apart from the millions of slaves, particularly in the south, whose presence disfigured all its ideals as Tocqueville observed, and who only became legally and constitutionally equal half a century ago. So there was no hereditary nobility, no peerage or formal gentry. All that really mattered was wealth and talent. From 'log cabin to White House' was the American equivalent of Dick Whittington with his cat setting out from the country and later becoming Lord Mayor of London. Yet the leap in America was even greater than in Britain.

There is a chapter in Claudio Veliz's *Gothic Fox* entitled 'A World Made in English'. What Veliz is alluding to is the fact that if a Martian visitor were to visit this planet he might well believe it had been designed by an Englishman. The world language is English; the world's widely copied political system is English democracy; the financial systems are largely English; market capitalism is a system that was invented in England; the world's leisure is dominated by English games; many civil society institutions from clubs to associations of many kinds derive from England; the legal system incorporated into both American and European law is largely English; the basis of most modern wealth producing processes, industrialisation and carbon-fueled energy, was invented in England; much of modern knowledge, from Newton to Crick and Watson, stems from England; the educational system in its top universities and schools has spread as a model over the world.

All this is true and it is important for a Chinese looking outwards to realise that, whether he is looking at cars or hamburgers, considering the role of law or personal rights, wanting to read some of the greatest poetry, novels and drama in the world, or interested in games and culture, he or she is often doing so by way of the small and peculiar island.

Now that the two-century dominance by the Anglosphere and Europe seems to be nearly over, it is timely to reassess and explore some of the deeper features of that legacy.

High Culture

One thing that strikes me is that, compared both to China and Europe, the Anglosphere has a curiously distorted artistic inheritance. If you want to look at great paintings you think of China or the Continent, for only a few Anglosphere artists are first class. Architecture is stronger and the English cathedrals are larger and more impressive than any others in the world, but sculpture and other forms of moulding are not as developed.

In music, the Anglosphere is a minor player. Compared particularly to the Germans and Austrians, who produced three quarters of the great classical musicians from Bach to Wagner, the only towering figure working in England was himself born in Germany, Handel. So in the plastic and expressive arts, a Chinese would look for style and brilliance outside the Anglosphere, just as he would look for the most sophisticated fashion, food and drink on the Continent.

Yet in one area the Anglosphere excelled. This was in literature and philosophy. The literature is incontestable. Even allowing for the dominance of English as a language, it would not be hard to maintain the view that three quarters of the great poets, from Shakespeare to T.S. Eliot were from the Anglosphere. Likewise, its novel writers, from Austen to Dickens, are world-class. I have often wondered why, not greatly distinguished in the plastic and visual arts, the British should excel in these fields and also, to a considerable extent in philosophy, essay writing and even detective fiction and ghost stories.

There are no doubt features of the English language which lend themselves to poetry and prose. English is both flexible and precise, endlessly changing and suitable for allusion and whimsy, rhythmic and haunting. The language is soaked in images from Shakespeare and the Jamesian translation of the Bible. It rings through the last half-millenium on the stage and in the mind. It is constantly branching into new explorations, nowadays in the richest creative centres of the world in film, television, satire and on the stage.

Yet I believe that it must be something more than just the good fortune of the language and its early glories. There has to be something absorbing to be said and that something has to address themes which matter through the ages and still resonate today. One way to approach this, spanning poetry and novels to children's literature, is to look at the two central preoccupations in this writing. When we do so, we see that they are themes which seem absolutely 'modern' and relevant to us today.

Love and loneliness

One of these is concerned with the agonies of love. Well over three quarters of the best of Anglosphere poetry, drama and novels are concerned with romantic love, the finding and uniting with, and possibly losing, the 'desired other'. Why should this be such an important subject?

Focusing on China, but also true of most civilisation, Confucian ideas do not rule out love, but love is not the basis for marriage. The Chinese system was not based on an equal, binding, love between two humans – the most powerful union in their lives, which became more important than the relations to parents or children. Such privileging of husband-and-wife relations seems unethical, selfish, an undermining of the hierarchical order. It is irrational, based on strange feelings and not on reason. What a crazy idea that you can leave the safety of birth-given dependence to find a partner, 'fall in love' with a total stranger, whatever that means, and hope to remain faithful to that person for the rest of your life.

Yet this is what the English did and from Anglo-Saxon times onwards their family system revolved around the love between husband and wife. A child would leave home as a servant, apprentice, schoolchild, at between eight and fourteen years old and live with strangers. He or she would lose the deep link to their parents, meet a total stranger, decide they 'loved' them, and fill the void created by the loss of parental bonds with a new union which was meant to be of body, soul and mind.

There are arguments about where and how 'romantic love' started, some tracing it to the troubadours of mediaeval France for example. Of course there are likely to be multiple origins, and love of a romantic kind is to be found in all societies. I have seen it in a remote Nepalese village where the boys and girls sing and flirt and sometimes run away to marry 'for love'.

Yet there are grounds for thinking that, as an institutional system, where love is tied to marriage and shapes all family relations, the 'romantic love complex' was principally developed, if not invented, in Britain. Certainly it is very old and has changed little for over a thousand years. It fits perfectly with a system of breaking up the family of parents and children, floating the children off into the wider stream of 'Society', independent participants in a wider economic, political, religious and social world which is not based on the family.

So a wave of love-related pressures flooded across the world, through advertising, marketing, art and entertainment. This challenged the parent-child primacy of most civilisations. The system of love marriage has to be understood as part of a basic shift from vertical (parent to child) to horizontal (husband to wife) family structures. The Anglosphere consists of individuals who are like molecules, early detached from their birth family and set 'free' to act as they personally feel is best.

The advantages of this system are seen in the human rights each person has, their democratic 'freedoms'. There is equality before the law, unusually equal relations between old and young, men and women, a freedom of religious opinion, free speech up to a point. This is all under the banner of 'Liberty and Equality'. The right to fall in love and place one's partner before one's parents and even one's own children is part of all this.

Yet it also has a cost. The 'Lonely Crowd', as David Riesman called it, refers to a world where each person is, ultimately, alone, Robinson Crusoe on his island, complete but separated from all others. Yet in love, as also in friendship there is the chance to open up and become whole again in relation to the mirror of the Other. The 'defects of loneliness' of which the poet John Donne wrote, are 'controlled' by love. Again, in Donne's famous phrase, 'no man is an island', even if the 'continent' to which we are joined is just one other person chosen through love.

The centrality of this emotional feature at the heart of the Anglosphere, making it very different from traditional China or India and pretty different from familistic systems on much of the Continent, cannot be stressed too much. It is even different from the Japanese case which, in its loneliness and separation might be thought to resemble the system. Yet the Japanese 'lobster pot' is too small to admit a stranger – the married partner perhaps becomes a friend, but always remains a stranger.

Friendship and clubs

Another feature of the Anglosphere world is the importance of non-family friendship. The movement of the individual from their birth family into a wider society does not happen in this way in any other great civilisation. It happens through socialization and the educational system. It means that one has a 'married friend', the special friend with whom one shares everything.

Most people also develop through much of their life other friendships, people with whom they like to spend time, share resources and contacts, engage in 'team activities'. These are enormously important. It would not be an exaggeration to call the Anglosphere the 'Friendship' civilisation, the very word 'friend' being derived from the Anglo-Saxon language.

In family-based civilisations, for example traditional China and Europe, most of one's important contacts, the people one trusts and work with, are related by blood or marriage. In the artificial kinship of Japan and the fragmented families of the Anglosphere, other principles have to be used to construct the ties which enable people to achieve their goals.

In Japan people create groups – businesses, manufacturing industries, agricultural farms – which have a flavour of the family, even if the members are not blood or marital relatives. So the big corporations and small shops feel like family firms – people feel mutual responsibility, trust each other, pool their resources, work closely together. In the Anglosphere the extension of family sentiment is not strongly present except in turning a stranger through marriage into a member of one's own inner core – a married friend.

Friendship has to be balanced. This is not the 'lopsided' friendship of patron-client ties, or of a father to a child, which are so important in Europe, especially in the Mediterranean countries or in the *jajmani* (patron-client) systems of India. In patronage systems, the social hierarchy is mirrored in religion, in the 'patron saints' and the Virgin Mary. They act as protectors, putting the individual in touch with resources and shielding him or her from threats.

Such a system is more or less absent, except in mild forms, in the Anglosphere. Instead, the child who enters society learns the art of meeting strangers and turning some of them into 'friends', finding some shared enthusiasm or attitude to life. Friends may provide minor economic or political support, but it is particularly the social and cultural closeness which gives many people much of the meaning in their life. 'Instrumental' friendship, using friends to achieve practical goals, often destroys a friendship.

Alongside this, and often providing the premise of friendship, is Associationalism. Tocqueville noted that a key to understanding America was the vast proliferation of non-kin associations, clubs and groups to do everything that a single individual could not do on their own. From religion, through economic to political or cultural activity, almost everything was done with another, non-related, individual or set of individuals in association. The equality and individualism of America made this even more important than it had been in the place of its origin, Britain, but it was in England that it had been developed over the centuries.

From Anglo-Saxon times onwards, formal legal and informal social customs had arisen to make it possible and desirable for individuals to overcome their separate impotency by joining with others. These groups, corporations of a kind, had an existence, a kind of artificial 'body' ('corporation', from corpus – a body in latin) with its own personality and even property. Most obviously this is expressed in the idea of the club. By the seventeenth century, when England shaped America, the home country had a wide proliferation of these civil society groupings which are the underpinning, as Tocqueville recognised, of an open economy and balanced democracy.

The law allowed the setting up of an artificial entity which acted like a person – with a name, right to hold property, rules of conduct, various assets – yet composed of a set of individuals who were voluntarily recruited to the group, not on the basis of blood or marriage, but on other grounds – merit, ability, interest, usefulness.

This institutional framework lay behind the organised development of most of the team games in the world, most famously football and cricket, but also everything from mountain climbing to athletics. It lay behind the invention of most of the early philanthropic organisations – the Red Cross, the Samaritans, the RSPCA the RSPCC. It under-pinned the development of the sciences, the Royal Society and the British Academy, of the theatres and museums, of the working men's clubs and the Trade Unions. It lay behind education, and in childhood the Boy Scouts and the Girl Guides.

Of course people associate for various purposes in all civilisations. Usually, however, as such associations become more powerful, they are viewed with suspicion by the State which tries to crush them. Thomas Hobbes in the *Leviathan* warned the rulers to crush the 'intestinal worms', as he called them, the Trusts which were eating away at the stomach of Royal rule.

Banned by the state, the associations tend to go underground, to become defined as criminal, at war with the state – the Triads of China, the Mafia of Sicily, and, more openly the bandits (*ban-diti* - Italian for outside the law) of many civilisations. One of the curiosities is that, on the whole, except on the margins or in immigrant groups, the Anglosphere has hardly developed this 'black' form of associational culture.

On the whole the State is feared and hated in most civilisations, keeping control through armies and armed police, crushing all dissent and any challenge, taxing as heavily as it can. In the Anglosphere, though there is grumbling, the protections of civil society and the feeling of being represented in the decisions of the state, means that the gulf is less. On the whole, the government, the police, the law are part of 'us', on our side, somewhat accountable to us.

The Common Law system is one where juries protect individuals by allowing the matter of guilt to be decided by one's peers, and not the State. To this day in England almost all of the criminal cases are dealt with by ordinary, voluntary and unpaid magistrates, members of the public acting as Justices of the Peace. This, again, protects people against arbitrary power.

Corruption and influence

Furthermore, in the absence of strong classes or castes, or of the older, powerful clans which have now been shattered, new methods of working with people on a daily basis have to be found. One of these in China, which it is difficult for a Westerner to understand since it does not seem to fit into either of the archetypal 'patronage' or 'friendship' models, is what is called *guanxi*. These are selected, often long-term, relations of mutual usefulness, sometimes mixed with some emotional liking. They should be balanced, and not too openly exploitative. They are similar to the 'friends of friends' that the anthropologist Jeremy Boissevain describes in his work on Malta.

They are networks of overlapping contacts and reciprocal exchanges. People in control of various resources exchange their access to these, often in indirect and disguised ways through mutual entertaining. The system allows such channels to exist and people to achieve complex goals by manipulating them. There is always the threat that, pushed too far, these can lead to what is often termed 'corruption', that is mixing of family, politics and economics which is a perpetual worry and supposedly endemic in many civilisations.

In terms of corruption, of course the Anglosphere has its own forms, the 'old boy network', the Masonic lodges, the buying of political favours and lobbying and pork-barrel politics. Yet, on the whole, the inhabitants of the Anglosphere believe that the mingling of family, politics and economics is less flagrant, because the definition of its modernity is that very separation between them.

Childhood and loss

Let me return to the question of why Britain created a great deal of the world's finest poetry, drama and children's stories.

As well as the turmoils of romantic love, there lies the fact that much of this literature is concerned with loss. There is a memory of something that once existed, a wholeness and integration that seems to vanish as one grows up.

From Edmund Spenser, through the metaphysical poets, by way of Pope and Gray, and obviously in full force with the Romantic poets up to Tennyson and Rupert Brooke, we have a long, sad, lingering farewell. As well as coming to terms with the loss of parental love, there is a feeling of deep regret at the loss of some kind of childhood experience of a more meaningful, spiritually rich, world. Even if that world, as in the books of Roald Dahl (who went to English schools), was pretty unpleasant in many ways, something is lost when one leaves it.

One famous expression is in the poetry of William Wordsworth, but before that, Milton's epic and aptly titled 'Paradise Lost', or William Blake, or, later, Tennyson's 'In Memoriam' or 'Morte d'Arthur' and certainly in much of W. B. Yeats' poetry and T. S. Eliot's 'Four Quartets', there is an overpowering grief at losing some interconnected, undivided, world of childhood with its attendant magic.

The theme is to be found in much of Anglosphere literature. We find it in *The Tempest* and *A Midsummer Night's Dream* through to the books for children. From *Alice in Wonderland*, through Rudyard Kipling's works, the stories of Beatrix Potter, A. A. Milne and Pooh, James Barry and Peter Pan never wanting to grow up, through to C. S. Lewis and Narnia and J. K. Rowling and Hogwarts. In all of them, there is a depiction of a magical world which lies outside this rather drab adult world. It can be entered through a tunnel, wardrobe, platform eight and three quarters. There are many other evocations of childhood, in autobiographies, novels such as *Cider with Rosie,* and many more.

Why is this such a powerful theme? A simple explanation

takes us back to 'modernity'. The life experience in the Anglosphere starts in the heart of a family, surrounded by strong feelings and an apparently undivided world. Parents, brothers and sisters and other close relatives dominate and there is no separation in our lives between head and heart. It is a world where one has no independent political, economic or social power. It is a landscape of myths and stories, mixing animals and humans, nature and culture, of Father Christmas and the tooth fairy, of dragons and demons, of magic and enchantment.

This tribal, integrated, world, in many ways not very different to that inhabited by most of humanity for many thousands of years, becomes eroded through life. At an early age you are taught to be independent, to think and act for yourself, to make your own decisions, to distance yourself, to exercise self-control, to divide your life into its separate parts. Schools teach this and the social system supports it. The whole process is outlined in an elegant way in John Locke's *Some Thoughts on Education* (1693) but it had existed in England long before and can be found in Shakespeare and earlier writers.

So you have to learn to be 'rational'. While imagination and fantasy continue in the make-believe worlds of art, games, reading or television, life as a whole is a place where you are on your own. You become Robinson Crusoe on his island, a single being except in relation perhaps to God. You may assuage this with love and friendship, but essentially the civilisation is based on individual atoms.

Given this life trajectory, where the meaning of life changes and a modern Anglosphere inhabitant becomes to a certain extent 'disenchanted', as Max Weber put it, it is not surprising that this should be reflected in great literature. It is the poets and novelists and children's story writers who have described it.

Struggle and play

The consequence of being part of a 'structural', relational world, as opposed to being within an atomistic, independent, individualistic civilisation are immense. One difference can be seen in the value of harmony as opposed to confrontation and struggle. In a structural civilisation of the kind I have tried to sketch, particularly in China, there are endless balances to be maintained. Every relationship and event involves its opposite and so the centre of Confucian thought is concerned with balance, agreement, consensus, mutual responsibility, adjustment.

If I compare this to what I observe in the Anglosphere we find something totally different. The point was well made by the Japanese philosopher Yukichi Fukuzawa when he tried to translate the central concept of market capitalism into the neo-Confucian ideas of Japan towards the end of the nineteenth century. He translated the western word 'free market' by two characters meaning 'race against' and 'fight'. He was reprimanded by his Confucian superiors for choosing such 'unpeaceful' words and told to choose something more harmonious. He pointed out that war, fighting and trying to beat someone in a race is exactly the essence of 'capitalism'. To change this into 'loving reciprocity', or 'duty to one's family and Emperor', as was suggested, would completely lose its meaning.

Western economics is based on competition. As Karl Marx observed, Charles Darwin's 'survival of the fittest' world can be seen as a projection onto the animal kingdom of what capitalism is about. The market is ethically neutral and the strongest, cleverest, most forceful, tend to succeed. The weak and indecisive are pushed to the edge. As in Tennyson's lament, in such a vision nature (including humans) is 'red in tooth and claw'.

I realised this as I went through my boarding education. The tough, competitive games I played at schools were to teach me how to defeat my opponents, within the rules of course. We learnt to 'fight' with marbles and chestnuts (conkers) and balls and whatever was at hand. We sensed that when we grew up we would fight with other weapons.

The Anglosphere has been almost constantly at military war since its inception and up to Iraq and beyond. Life is a never-ending struggle, both against one's own base emotions and against others, as my two school mottoes reminded me. The first was *Per Ardua ad Solem* ('by struggling, try to reach the sun'), the second was *Dura Virum Nutrix* ('a hard or tough nurse of men'.)

The Common Law system is all about fighting with words, oppositional and aggressive in both civil and criminal courts. Politics is also confrontational. Again Fukuzawa from Japan was appalled to hear the apparent aggression in the House of Commons when he visited it. Yet he also noted that when they walked from the 'theatre' of the house, the apparent 'enemies', who had been threatening to kill each other, went off for a friendly drink together.

Fukuzawa realized quickly that what softened this endless aggressive confrontation, this attempt to break down harmony, to separate and win minor victories, was the fact that it was all, in the end, a game. 'Fair play', that is competing as hard as possible for temporary victories, creating inequality, making a superior and inferior in an economic transaction, law case, political argument, or game of football, was 'just a game'. It did not create permanent inequality. After the game was over, the tussle with the pillows or with golf clubs or stocks and shares or parliamentary debates, your friendship might become deeper, the recognition of a mutual respect was enforced.

We can see it all the time in the greatest English writer, Shakespeare, whose 'players' are indeed full of confrontational play. Yet it is limited and controlled play. This is particularly true of the main form of play, language. Even apparently physical play, team games and sports are also, of course, simultaneously mental play. The majority of playing occurs in language and in particular in humour.

When I came to look again at what I learnt at school, I was amazed to find how much attention was paid to learning about humour. I studied and sometimes acted in the musicals and plays of the great humourists – Gilbert and Sullivan, Bernard Shaw, Oscar Wilde, or the comedies of Shakespeare, or read the great satirical poetry of Dryden and Pope. I learnt how to use wit – irony, satire, double meanings, the under and over statement. I learnt that all was susceptible to the approach of great satirical radio and television programmes, 'The Goons', 'Monty Python', 'Dad's Army', 'The League of Gentlemen', 'Blackadder'.

Humour, like myth, is a way of dealing with inconsistencies, contradictions, pain and pathos. The British have been renowned for facing up to hardship with a quip 'you've got to laugh'. With the ubiquitous cup of tea at hand, they laughed at Hitler and Mussolini, and they also laughed at their monarchs, prime ministers, their toffs and their bishops. Above all they laughed at themselves.

Thus, although the humour changed somewhat when it went to America, it was also exported to India and other parts of the Empire. Some would argue that alongside industrialism, capitalism, the English language and literature, English law, games, English democracy, we should place English humour and self-mockery as one of the greatest contributions made by this insignificant island off the coast of Europe. It was a humour which help to preserve the flame of liberty, elsewhere exterminated all over Europe only seventy years ago.

A modern world

We can define the 'modern' as a world where the four great forces – belief, wealth, society and power – have, in theory, been separated into discrete institutional spheres. It is not based on birth groups or on fundamental relationships – it is individualistic and not 'structural'. It is held together by constant competition between separate individuals, but it is a competition which also allows them to form into very strong quasi-groups or associations based on choice.

A defining characteristic of this modernity is its restlessness, arising from the insecurity and anxiety of individuals never sure of their fate and salvation either here on earth or in the after-world. Yet with all its obsession with money as the only true marker and guarantee of status, its disinterest or philistinism in relation to many of the arts, its puritanism and its loneliness, it was and is powerful.

As it contacted the pre-existing great civilisations that grew up from Confucius in the East, Hinduism and Buddhism in India, the Persians and Middle Eastern Prophets and the Greek philosophers transmuted through Rome into Europe, the Anglosphere presented a rather unusual and unexpected new form. No one would have predicted that a small, rather damp, backward and remote island would invent so much of our modern world. Who could have guessed five hundred years ago that this small island would set many of the terms of the international exchange in our global network, from the banks and industries, to the culture, language, games and associations.

Civilisations Compared

Wealth and Poverty

To THE HOLIDAY maker or business-man, Shanghai, Tokyo, Berlin or London seem much the same. The cars, factories, clothes, food, popular culture, televisions, computers, stock exchanges look similar. It is easy to believe that it has long been thus. It is also easy to be lulled into the easy assumption that the inner spirit behind each civilisation's material world is much the same.

Yet this would be wrong. Although there has been a convergence in the last thirty years, any part of the world we encounter is a meeting of civilisations which have come along different paths, and whose inner spirit is still, in many ways, a long way apart. The forces that have shaped them are the result of particular and very different ecologies, geographies, demographies, technologies, as well as political, social, intellectual and religious systems.

Geography and ecology

Perhaps the deepest conditioning factor is geography. The rivers, mountains, soil and climate do not absolutely determine anything, yet they permit or encourage certain features in a civilisation. Several things stand out when we look at the civilisations together. One is that large, flat, landmasses like China, central Europe or parts of the Middle East, with less access to the sea and with long land borders, tend to lead to empires and authoritarian governments to control the borders. The threat of attacks means that the central powers can blackmail their nobility and peasants into servility.

On the other hand, it is no coincidence that the two cases of a particular form of dispersed power, known as 'centralised feudalism', a strong centre but also powerful countervailing forces in a military aristocracy, should be found on two large islands at opposite ends of Eurasia, Japan and Britain.

Tocqueville described how being an island, and at that time he included North America, with no powerful land enemies allowed a quasi-democratic balance of powers to flourish. Yet the island had to be large enough; an island such as Venice or the other Italian city states, and even Holland after its great age, was not large enough to maintain its independence.

Such island-hood would also allow a civilisation to incubate and protect an increasingly different and unusual social structure, in many respects totally the opposite of that of the large neighbouring civilisation, as we have again seen in Japan and Britain.

The soil and climate also tend to affect much else through the nature of the crops that are grown. Montesquieu pointed to the great difference between the Mediterranean olive and grape area in the south and the wheat and apples of the north. The lighter soils of the south favoured the scratch plough of the Romans and the deep soils of the North the heavy wheeled plough of the Germans. These different ploughs lead to different field shapes which led to different village shapes which led to different social structures and mentalities.

Likewise the huge difference of intensive rice cultivation in East Asia and South India and the wheat and hard grains of northern China, northern India and the West are also obvious in terms of technology, social structure and politics. For example, there is a tendency for rice cultivators to concentrate on the increase of human labour and its greater efficiency. This leads towards a 'high level trap' as cheap labour pushes out animals, and it leads away from machinery. Extensive, hard

grain, production, on the other hand, encourages the supple-
mentation of human labour by animals and machines. Neither
is inevitable, but many of the differences between the history
of southern China and Japan on the one hand, and Europe
and the Anglosphere on the other, can be partially explained
as a contrast between the world of rice and the world of wheat.

'Fat' and 'Thin' civilisations

We can broadly contrast two kinds of historical civilisation
– the 'fat' and the 'thin'. Although the distinction is less obvious
today, particularly to those who live in modern 'fat' civilisations, it was very clear to our predecessors. For example, it was
the explicit theme of many English cartoons of the eighteenth
century, which contrasted the fat, well-dressed, meat-eating
and beer-drinking English with the thin, dressed-in-rags, half-
starved, vegetarian and water-drinking counterparts in France.

There seems to be a real contrast between the Anglosphere
on the one hand and the other civilisations on the other. Travellers through the Celtic fringe (Ireland, Scotland and Wales)
of Britain, and most of Continental Europe (Holland was a
conspicuous exception) from the sixteenth century onwards
noticed that in terms of housing, clothing and food, the
English middling sort seemed increasingly fortunate.

Their houses were substantially built. I live in such a house,
half of a small seventeenth century farmer's cottage in one of
the poorest areas of England. With its oak beams and flooring,
solid walls, thick thatch, firm foundations and individual well,
it is a house to be proud of even to this day.

Many English villages contain substantial late mediaeval
and early modern houses, whereas if you travel through the
continent or the Celtic fringe, Japan and China, or much of
the Middle East, outside the richer parts of cities, you will

find hardly any ordinary people's houses much older than a hundred years. This is partly due to climate, war and building materials, but also to the amount of disposable wealth of ordinary people which they could use, with confidence, on their housing. The English homes are still often filled with substantial and comfortable furniture, dating back hundreds of years, which hardly exists at the village level elsewhere in the world.

Likewise many travellers before the twentieth century, travelling from England or North America to most of the rest of the world, including continental Europe, Japan and China, noticed the difference in food. Compared to their own substantial high protein diets of milk, cheese, butter and meat, the 'peasants' of other civilisations, including the Scotland visited by Dr Johnson in the later eighteenth century, seemed impoverished. The vast majority of the population subsisted mainly on inferior grains and a thin assortment of vegetables.

In the seventeenth century, the English could afford to turn half their grain harvest into a drink – beer, which was drunk every day by all the population – while most people in other civilisations could only drink small amounts of plant-produced alcohol (including wine) on special occasions, so that the normal drink was water, as in Islam, or tea in parts of Japan and China.

The contrast between 'fat' and 'thin' clearly mirrors other differences in economy and social structure. Peasants in most civilisations tended to live very close to the subsistence level. Any surpluses were quickly absorbed and it is only on special feast days or at weddings and other special events that richer foods, drinks and clothing might appear. There is a vast literature to describe such a situation in Italy, Spain, France and Russia, just as there is in India and China.

The meagre situation presses people to be enormously economical, as were the Japanese and Chinese, never 'wasting' anything, from human excrement to scraps of food or clothing. This is something which the prodigal Anglosphere hardly comprehends.

This explains many differences even to this day, for example in relation to animals. The English have often been shocked that the Chinese appear, in the past, to have eaten almost anything, from dogs and cats, to snakes and rats and all kinds of birds.

The differences reflect a contrast between famine-prone and subsistence-struggling peasants on the one hand, and those who can afford to leave a little of nature free because they have more than enough from their productive agriculture. The immensely hard, careful, world of agriculture, in contrast to the destruction of the wider environment, is a problem with which China and much of the world is currently struggling. It reflects something importantly different in the realm of concepts of property which distinguishes the Anglosphere from the other examples. It is a difference of great significance in our present world, where the destruction of forests and oceans through over-exploitation is one of the central features.

Private and public property

In almost all civilisations there is an absolute distinction between assets which are owned by an individual, or a bounded group of individuals (for example jointly by a family), and those which are 'common', that is free for all to exploit. Often the privately owned assets are bounded in some way, with a wall or fence in the case of land, or markers and labels in the case of animals. The private assets are not to be shared beyond the individual or the small group which has invested time, labour or money in their acquisition and development, or inherited them.

On the other hand, the forests, mountain pastures, rivers and seas are open to all those who are within their reach, to use as fully as they can. The so-called 'Tragedy of the Commons' refers to the fact that across the world nowadays the category of the Commons leads to the denuding of the mountains, the emptying of the rivers and seas and their use as dustbins which can be degraded and polluted as a 'free' resource by those who wish to do so. This destruction, whereby 'wild' or 'common' nature is 'free' to all, is one factor in the destruction of wildlife. The desperate or merely playful peasants will descend on any common resource and chop, kill and exploit what they can.

The Anglosphere has developed a more complex, three-way, distinction of property from mediaeval times, which explains not only the preservation of much wildlife and the founding of most of the nature conservancy bodies within the Anglosphere (with societies to protect animals, birds, parks, moors, old houses, mountains and oceans) but also the prevalence of many 'community' resources.

We can easily detect such 'communally' owned resources in the Anglosphere by looking out for the use of the word 'public' (which is misleading, since they are not 'public' at all as we shall see) as an adjective preceding a resource. So we have public parks, libraries, toilets, footpaths and bridleways. This curious intermediate, third way, concept of half-private, half-public, property is little understood. It is worth explaining how it works.

There was in mediaeval England, a legal concept that some things are entirely private, owned by an individual and not to be taken from him or her without his or her agreement. This included a person's body, rights of free expression and many other 'human rights' (or 'liberties' as they were called in those days).

This idea of innate 'human rights' is now, of course, used

all the time, but no-one outside the Anglosphere would have endorsed it or known what it meant before a couple of hundred years ago. Normally, in other civilisations, a person has no innate and absolute rights as an individual – just a set of reciprocal rights and obligations in relation to one or more others. There was no absolute private ownership, either over yourself or any other assets.

Such an extreme form of individual liberty or rights in the Anglosphere would have led to a totally dysfunctional, atomistic, society if it had not been balanced by a mechanism to allow individuals to share resources in some kind of semi-communal system. In the same way as playing a team game involves individual rights and initiatives, combined with 'team' obligations, so there was developed a system to allow property to be both private and public, or blended.

One way to demonstrate what this means is to look at the idea of the 'commons' in an English village over the last thousand years, and still present today in the small Cambridgeshire village where I live. In all English villages, there were in the past smaller or greater 'common' resources. These might be an area of common grazing on the fields or fells, or common forestry in the woods, or common fishing rights in the local river, or 'public' rights of way.

At first sight this looks like a recipe for the tragedy. People would take out their sheep or pigs onto these 'commons', cut wood in the forests, fish in the common streams or lakes. Yet when we examine the arrangements more closely we see that they were not 'common' in the sense of being open to all to do what they wanted there.

Thus a passing stranger, entering an English village with a horse or axe or fishing rod would quickly be stopped from using such assets – it was poaching or trespassing. Certain groups, from a different tradition, particularly gypsies, cause tension in England since they often do not recognize these limitations.

In fact, over the centuries, these rights were strictly regulated and derived from membership of a particular village. A land-holding or house would give you rights to 'stint' (the old English word) a certain number of animals on the communal grazing. Or, as I found with the small house where I lived in the Yorkshire moors, it gave me the right to cut a certain number of peats on the moor. Or you might have the right to catch and keep a certain number of fish over a certain size from a particular river or pond.

All these rights were preserved, supervised and policed; there were beck watchers, fell watchers, forest watchers appointed by and acting on behalf of those who held the common resource. It is this which preserved nature, plus the strong hunting, shooting, fishing monopolies of those who had bought or inherited such rights.

This intermediary 'in common but not universally free', concept, coming out of old Germanic law and totally at odds with traditional continental Roman law, or the law of China and Japan, is of crucial importance today. A growing application of the principal will also help us to preserve the last of the rainforests, the mango groves, the oceans and the polluted rivers from total destruction. They are now to be preserved as 'commons' for all inhabitants on earth, but that does not mean we can freely plunder them.

All this links back to the topic of 'fat' and 'thin' in diverse ways. Setting up a system whereby people could join together in contractual communities, benefitting from each other's efforts but also restraining behaviour to their mutual advantage, allows wealth to steadily increase. A 'fellowship' or 'village community' or team or club can join in the enjoyment of a shared resource, which is not partitioned among them, and which they securely use under a set of agreed rules.

Such an organization, which lies between the individual and the state, and is the basis of civil society, is one of the mechanisms which helped to make the Anglosphere into the first 'fat' civilisation. Its extension elsewhere is gradually, at least at present, lifting many of the 'thin' into modest affluence.

Peasants and petty capitalists

The vast majority of the inhabitants in the four civilisations covered here lived out their lives on the land as rural cultivators. Hundreds and sometimes thousands of years trying to earn a living off agriculture still influences mentalities and moralities to this day.

A very widespread form of rural society and economy is described as 'peasant', coming from the French for country person (*paysan*). Peasants have formed most of the inhabitants of the great agrarian civilisations over the last two thousand years, from Europe, Russia and India, to South America, South East Asia and China.

The essence of such peasantry is what some analysts have termed 'The Domestic Mode of Production'. The unit of production and consumption and the family unit (based on the household or 'domestos') are identical. The land is worked and owned not by paid individuals, as in modern farming, but by family labour. The head of the household is also the director of the farming enterprise. The complex includes the shared rights given by birth, where most of the production is for internal consumption within the family, with little being sold or traded, though there may be bi-occupations.

Such a model of peasantry, consisting of the overlap of the basic social and basic economic units in the countryside, fits pretty well with two of our four cases, namely China, and continental Europe. Until very recently, both were peasant societies, with little penetration of a wider money economy, little social mobility, no individualized property. The classic account of China in the works of its leading anthropologist, Fei Hsiao-Tung, describes this world and there are numerous works by anthropologists and novelists describing a similar peasant world in traditional Europe and Islamic civilisations.

It might be imagined that such would be the situation in all societies before modern industrialization and urbanization. It is easy to assume that it is the inevitable stage between early 'tribal' and recent 'modern' societies. Such was the sequence of civilisations suggested, for example, by Karl Marx and Max Weber, and early in my life I, like others, accepted the sequence.

Yet when I came to examine the original documents for English rural society from the thirteenth century onwards, I discovered that in this definition, England had never been a peasant society. The property system, the separation of economy and society, the mobility of workers, the penetration of money values, meant that England was different.

It is difficult to know what to call the unusual English structure, but something like 'proto-capitalist' might fit. The supposed 'capitalist revolution', accepted by many since the writing of Marx, never occurred in England. There is no dramatic and revolutionary change from one 'mode of production' to another.

Since America and the wider Anglosphere inherited this unusual structure, emerging when it was already well in place in the sixteenth century, this non-peasant social and economic situation is now to be found in all the white areas of the Anglosphere. Of course the English could not impose it over their mainly native Empire in India, Burma and elsewhere, though through their laws and administration they introduced some elements of it. Yet it is the basic structure of the Anglo-American system for the last centuries.

The other civilisation, Japan, appears to be, perhaps surprisingly, on the side of the Anglosphere in this respect. All that we know of the centralized feudal system in Japan, the artificiality of its family, the high mobility, the penetration of money and market values, indicates that on that other island civilisation, there was also an unusual and exceptional, non-peasant, social structure. So the break between economy and society, which Weber considered to be the quintessence of a free market and hence to allow 'rational' capitalism to emerge, was also present very early.

So we have two groups of civilisations in terms of their basic social structures. China and Europe have evolved through the structures of peasantry, deeply based on family relations. The Anglosphere, at least in its white settler areas, and Japan, have not had the peasant formation, though of course there were many rural dwellers.

The consequences of this difference extends far beyond the social, economic and even demographic patterns. It affects the nature of politics, religion and ideology. It is a cause of much of what appears to be strangely different when we compare the first industrial nation of the West (Britain) and the East (Japan) as compared to their neighbouring continental neighbours, Europe and China.

Crisis and balanced populations

Our four civilisations now have more or less balanced populations, with low birth and death rates leading to a more or less constant number of people. They have reached this position along very different paths. Those paths are worth understanding for they have had a great effect on the deeper mentality, morality, social systems and economies of the four cases. The effects reverberate to this day, most dramatically in the 'One Child Policy' introduced in China in 1978 and only now being gradually phased out. The effects are also to be seen in debates about abortion and contraception in the Anglo-sphere and on marital behaviour in Japan.

We can divide the population patterns in civilisations over the last thousand years into two major kinds. One may be termed a 'crisis' model. Here, in normal years, there is a high fertility rate. Women marry young, have as many children as possible, and as a result, each couple will have up to six or eight children or more.

Quite large numbers of the infants and women die early, but as long as death rates are reasonably low the population will grow fast, easily doubling each generation. So the population grows rapidly for one or more generations and then characteristically a 'crisis' occurs. This consists of one or more of the terrible events described by the eighteenth century economist, Thomas Malthus, that is War, Famine and Disease. In such a crisis the population may be halved. Then it begins to grows at an ever increasing rate again.

In such a crisis pattern, people want as many children as possible. They need them for labour in the fields. Since the unit of production and the unit of reproduction is the same in a peasant society, the more children you have the better your family farm economy will work. The safest thing to invest in, to protect you against the risks and hazards of sickness, accident and old age, is a large family.

There are often religious reasons why many children are desired. The ancestors are pleased; the God or gods are pleased; merit is achieved. Families with large numbers of children become wealthier and in the insecure political struggles of village life, a big family becomes more powerful. It is essential to marry off one's daughters as young as possible and to find good brides for one's sons. A family without many children has low status and a woman who does not have children has no status at all.

This crisis pattern is the one we find in the peasant civilisations of China and much of continental Europe, but not the Anglosphere, until very recently. If we were to look at a graph of the long-term trends in Chinese, Egyptian, French or Spanish population, we would find that it shows spurts of growth, with a doubling of the total population in each generation. Then, suddenly, there is a shattering fall, with perhaps a quarter or more of the population dying.

The worst crisis is widespread warfare, for this often brings with it the closely connected disasters of famine and epidemic disease. So the periodic devastating wars in China, particularly the Mongol invasion, which may have led to the death of up to a quarter or a third of the Chinese population, are examples of this pattern. The same is true in Europe where, for example, the Thirty Years War of the seventeenth century is estimated to have led to the deaths of up to a quarter or a third of the German population.

Standing back, we see that until relatively recently, the majority of the huge peasant populations of much of the world, particularly in China, India, Russia and Continental Europe lived in a world where periodically there would be devastating events — millions would die of plague, famine or war. Here the family and many children were the only, very partial, protection against terrible catastrophes, the memory of which were passed on from generation to generation.

Such a world of terrible suffering has only very recently disappeared in these large peasant civilisations. The last mass famines and crises occurred in Russia during the 1930s and 1940s. They occurred in China in the 1940s to the 1960s, and in India during the same period. Although Continental Europe, apart from the devastations of the two World Wars, had escaped from much of this a little earlier in the second half of the nineteenth century, the memories were still present. Life was a struggle, catastrophe never far away.

The change from such a pattern is known as the 'demographic transition'. For reasons which are still little understood, in most countries in the world the maximum fertility of women began to be reduced through rising age at marriage and/or the use of contraception.

The most dramatic example is the Chinese 'One Child Policy', but all over continental Europe in the later nineteenth century something similar happened. Despite continued pro-natalist urging, despite the banning of all contraception and other forms of birth control by the Catholic Church, the fertility rate dropped dramatically throughout Italy, Spain, France and Germany about a hundred and fifty years ago. Then, some fifty years ago the transition spread across South America and much of Asia, though not parts of the Islamic world and sub-Saharan Africa.

The rising expectation of life accompanying a medical revolution, the education of women, the move from agriculture, where human labour is key to wealth production, to an industrial type of production, are all factors. Whatever the reasons, we currently live in a post-crisis pattern in much of the world. Yet there are certain groups, particularly amongst the strictest and most extreme members of the monotheistic religions – Jewish, Islamic and Christian – which maintain high natural fertility. They follow the exhortation to go forth and multiply, to spread God's word through the multiplication of the devout.

It was long thought that the demographic transition was a recent, two hundred year old at the most, phenomenon. It seemed to make sense to believe that before the industrial era of factory production, and the widespread perceived benefits of modern medicine, all agrarian societies had a similar pattern of high fertility and mortality and rocketing populations.

So powerful was this general assumption that in his famous *Essay on the Principle of Population* (1798), Thomas Malthus assumed that this was the case everywhere. He showed that natural fertility and normal mortality was such that population will grow exponentially: 1:2:4:8:16. Only about 34 doublings of this kind are needed to get from Adam and Eve to our present world population of over seven and a third billion. Malthus rightly believed that on the basis of the agricultural and manufacturing technologies of his time, economic growth could only be, at the best, arithmetic: 1:2:3:4. So he predicted disaster – the calamities of War, Famine and Disease would inevitably cut population growth back.

Yet, after his first short essay, Malthus undertook a great deal of research on the population patterns of many parts of the world, including China, the Pacific, the Continent, Ireland, England and Norway. What he discovered and described in the far larger second edition of *The Principle* five years later was a new theory in a new book. He showed that, in fact, the demographic transition had already occurred in certain countries, not through contraception but through the institution of marriage.

Particularly in Switzerland, Norway and England, factors such as clearly bounded resources, relative peace and an absence of famine, were behind another pattern. This is what we may call a homeostatic (homoeostasis being an automatic feedback mechanism) to keep a system in balance.

Here the major control is fertility, not periodic high

mortality. Even in the presence of plentiful resources of food and housing, people regulate their breeding as a result of social and economic pressures. In such a system people are not put under huge pressure to marry early or at all. When they do marry they may have only a few children. In such a case, with normal mortality, the population hardly grows in average years. It is kept in balance not by mortality crises but by people's desire to restrain their reproduction.

This is the pattern which characterised England from the mediaeval period onwards. We know, for example, that in the four hundred years between the Black Death in 1350 and the start of a new burst of population growth in the early Industrial Revolution around 1750, the wealth of England increased year by year. By the end of that crucial build-up of the infrastructure and general standard of living, people in England were perhaps three or four times richer than at the start of the period.

Yet in that same period the population had grown very slowly – perhaps doubling at most. There was a 'homeostatic' pattern where people put their increasing wealth into consumption rather than reproduction. As Malthus pointed out, people waited to marry until, as independent individuals, they could 'afford' to do so. They could not depend on their families to set them up, and came under no great pressure to marry. Up to a quarter of women never married at all, and the average age at first marriage was about ten years after puberty.

This controlled fertility pattern was taken to North America, and is also the one which has recently been described for Japan. Perhaps because of a similar absence of a peasant or 'domestic mode of production' which connects family size to family wealth, and a similar absence of a serious perennial threat of invading armies and hence war, famine and disease, the protected island of Japan had a similar population pattern to England.

The Japanese population reached a similar plateau in the two hundred and fifty years before its rapid industrial takeoff in the later nineteenth century. While the Japanese economy steadily grew and more than doubled in size, there was hardly any growth in the absolute population from the early seventeenth to mid nineteenth centuries. This was not because of war, famine and disease, but because Japanese families were relatively small.

The methods to make them just large enough to keep population static, but not to make it grow fast, were different from those in England. In England it was late and selective marriage which reduced fertility. In Japan marriages were not as late, and most women married, but there was much more use of various techniques to reduce the number of children, including abortion and infanticide. Yet different techniques led to the same outcome. Like England, surplus wealth was invested in improving standards of life, rather than in maximizing the number of children.

Industrious and Industrial Civilisations

The Japanese economic historian, Akira Hayami, suggested some years ago that one of the basic contrasts in recent history was between what he termed 'industrious' and 'industrial' patterns. He argued that Japan in the three centuries before its industrialisation in the later nineteenth century, had followed the 'industrious' path, while Britain in the three centuries up to its mid-eighteenth century breakthrough, had followed an 'industrial' road.

In the 'industrious' model, economic growth is achieved by hard and efficient human labour. Almost everyone, including women and children, push themselves ever harder to produce agricultural and craft goods, to increase their wealth, or to stave off disaster. Gains in productivity, particularly in rice farming, are made by double or triple cropping, planting vegetables in between other crops, using every piece of possible human and other fertilizing agent, harvesting every scrap of food.

Nothing is wasted and people are constantly on the lookout for ways to make small marginal increases through extra effort. People work almost non-stop, and if they do have time away from the agricultural work, they use it to repair their simple tools and in by-occupations such as weaving, pottery or basketwork to earn a little extra cash.

The 'industrial' path is different. Here we find that humans do not work harder with their bodies, but increasingly use non-human means of production. Later such industrial production is synonymous with factories, steam power, machines, the division of labour. Yet centuries before that occurred, a quasi-industrial system had been developing which dramatically increased production through harnessing the four forms of energy widely available – wind, water, animals and coal.

What the English did from the mediaeval period onwards was to develop all these forms of non-human energy. Animals were increasingly used, whether for ploughing (with the more efficient horse replacing oxen), or for converting plants into food and clothing. England became the most advanced animal-based economy in the world, filled with sheep, cows, pigs, horses and chickens. Each Englishman lived off the work of many animals.

This was a complete contrast to the industrious path where, for example in Japan, the number of animals decreased year by year so that by the middle of the nineteenth century there were hardly any domesticated animals in Japan at all, apart from a few small horses.

In England there was an extensive use of water power from the eleventh century onwards, with almost every household within reach of a reasonably sized mill to grind their corn. In Japan all the grinding was done by hand (querns) or by foot (rice pounders). In England, if there was not sufficient water power available, as in much of East Anglia, then from the thirteenth century there was the development of a widespread use of wind power, with many villages in England having one or two large windmills. Windmills of that scale and kind were hardly used in Japan.

Finally, over the last thousand years, the English started to develop an extensive use of fossil fuels, particularly coal. By the sixteenth century coal was very widely used and by the early eighteenth century each inhabitant in England, on average, had two or three invisible 'helpers' in the shape of coal energy to produce heat, power small industries and produce lime and other fertilizer for the fields. There was the largest coal production anywhere in the world. None of this happened in Japan, although later coal was to be discovered quite widely.

So we have two patterns on these two islands. The Japanese case is a form of 'agricultural involution', as Clifford Geertz the anthropologist calls it for Java. Here people work harder and harder and the cheapness of their labour, and the necessity to use every scrap of land to grow crops, drives out all non-human energy – animals and machines.

If we look at our other civilisations there are naturally some exceptions, but in general they fall decidedly on the side of industriousness. Clearly in a huge civilisation like China there are areas, in particular the one percent of the population who lived in the Yangtze and Yellow River deltas, where there was quite extensive use of machinery and division of labour. Yet on the whole, in most of China, the situation was similar to Japan.

China, to a certain extent like Japan moved away from potential industry to industriousness. The Chinese had early invented a kind of power loom, they used machines for controlling and using the power of the mighty rivers and also some wind power for producing salt. There was also some use of animals, particularly buffaloes, horses and pigs and quite extensive use of coal to smelt iron ore. All this was well developed by the thirteenth century in the Song dynasties. At that time, when Marco Polo visited, it looked as if China might develop towards the industrial path. Yet five hundred years later it had not moved further. There were less animals, the output of iron from coal firing had declined, the use of water and wind power had, if anything, shrunk.

There are many possible reasons for this. The cheapness of labour with rapid population growth and the difficulty of using non-human power in rice cultivation are among them. Whatever the reasons, it is clear that China by the nineteenth century was a classic 'industrious' civilisation. As most observers noticed, the people worked incredibly hard and efficiently, but almost all of the burden in the economy was carried by humans using their backs, arms and legs. There was little aid from nonhuman sources of energy or machinery.

We might expect that continental Europe would have been much closer to the English model, that the west in general moved together towards industrialization, not merely in England and the wider Anglosphere where its system was adopted, but also throughout the highly sophisticated cultures of Europe. Yet if we compare descriptions of late mediaeval agriculture and industry through Europe with what happened later, the pattern seems very similar to China.

The widespread machines and animals of medieval and early modern Europe remind us of Song China. Yet, once again, descriptions some centuries later show a similar trend to that of China. Much of Europe, particularly Italy, Spain and France seem to have retreated from their proto-industrial past.

Animals became scarcer in the general population. The peasants were using spades and hoes rather than animal-drawn ploughs. The use of coal had not increased. The use of wind and water power, apart from navigation, had not been extended. On the whole, the peasants were working ever harder as the fertility of their fields declined and the forests were thinned. They had to work longer hours to produce the same amount and to keep up with growing population and ever higher taxes. Much of continental Europe seemed to have reached a high level trap, or equilibrium or, as Adam Smith noticed in the eighteenth century, even to be declining.

Thus we have one path which affected three of the civilisations, Japan, China and continental Europe. In the half millennium before the nineteenth century they were increasingly following the industrious path. This strategy is one which is ultimately bound to lead to a dead end for it cannot use increasing reliable knowledge and the power of nonhuman technology to grow exponentially. Harvesting the energy of the sun solely through plants and human hard work confines production severely. It leads to a kind of self-inflicted slavery, a life of endless toil and grinding work.

Inward and outward looking civilisations

It is worth briefly considering one further major distinction between the four civilisations. This concerns the degree to which they are inward or outward looking in their economic systems. In this respect, we can see that both China and Japan were inward looking and Europe and the Anglosphere were outward looking. What I mean can be seen if we concentrate in particular on the Chinese case.

Although, or perhaps because, China is so vast and diverse, it has always had a problem of understanding and dealing with the non-Chinese 'stranger'. For most members of the Middle Kingdom, through most of history, people from other civilisations were barbarians of whom one might have heard, but with whom one had no contact. This tendency of huge civilisations to be largely ignorant of, and disinterested in, the rest of the world can be seen in the United States today. Surveys have shown that knowledge of the rest of the world, or even the possession of a passport to travel outside the States, is relatively unusual.

This inward-looking tendency was exacerbated in the Chinese case by several factors. One was that, from very early on, economic activity - trading, marketing, manufacture, making money, was looked down upon by the elite. Both the Legalists and Confucians, in different ways and for different reasons, placed economic activity by ordinary people at a low level in the social order. Too obviously pursuing money-making in a Mandarin society was demeaning. In the absence of corporate law and in the presence of a powerful government which would seize and tax any conspicuous wealth, large money-making endeavours were difficult to establish. Though there was a vast amount of petty commodity trading in many parts of China, especially on the East coast, large companies for trade and manufacture were conspicuous by their absence through most of Chinese history.

This was combined with the possibilities for a huge internal, small-scale, trade on the immense water-networks within China and the turning away from the possibility of overseas sea trading after the early fifteenth century. When we add in the fact that the two great waves of invaders who established Empires in China, the Mongols and the Manchus, were inland peoples with little experience or interest in maritime or even land trade, we can see the pressures against the development of the patterns we find in western Europe.

The effect was that the overseas trade of China was largely in the hands of people from other civilisations, intermediaries who controlled the exports of silk, porcelain, paper and tea. Along the land silk roads these were early on the Sogdians and the Muslim traders. On the sea silk roads and to Japan they were first the Arab traders and later the Portuguese (from 1515) and other western traders.

All of this became particularly important as the power of the western nations grew. It soon became apparent that the Chinese government did not really know how to handle the outside traders, except in a rather rigid and formal manner. Hence the incomprehension when Lord Macartney brought a trade mission from Britain in 1792, then the tragedy of the Opium Wars, and later misunderstandings. It is not surprising that the Chinese turned to the British expert Sir Robert Hart to organize and oversee their maritime customs system from the middle of the nineteenth century.

Power, Society and Ideas

Law

As DESCRIBED IN earlier chapters, complex and instituted legal systems, criminal and civil, have been traditionally more or less absent in two civilisations – China and Japan – and have been highly developed in Europe and the Anglosphere. Although this is changing rapidly in China nowadays, as it did in Japan in the twentieth century, the basic difference is between two kinds of legal order.

At the Sino-Japanese end, law was not needed except at the margins. Conflict resolution and civil disputes were largely dealt with by non-legal processes. The Western tradition, whether of the Roman Law area of the Continent or the Common Law of the Anglosphere, were at the opposite extreme. Sophisticated systems were developed around property, human relations, deviance, to deal with the clash of interests and actions. Law was needed to provide checks and balances and to separate out the individual from outside pressures.

China and Japan as they move to a situation where the traditional closeness is partly undermined by rapid urbanization and where they hope to import many Western technologies, educational ideas, economic institutions, are faced with the problem of how far to go down the road towards the litigation-soaked West.

The Japanese in their characteristic way have solved the problem by apparently absorbing the western paraphernalia. How far China will go in the Western direction is not yet certain. Certainly, my visits to Chinese law courts and talking to judges gives me a sense that China will absorb much more of the Western framework than Japan. Yet I suspect that, as time passes, it will evolve a new hybrid version – 'Western law with Chinese characteristics'.

For example, I am not sure that the jury system will ever take off in China – just as it has failed to take off in Japan. I suspect that the huge ratio of lawyers to population which we find in America, or the obsession with prosecuting for money, or the strong assertion of 'human rights' without the counter-balancing 'human responsibilities' will only partly be transported to China. There will be much more of a family flavour to the law, encouraging respect and duties to relatives.

Politics

The political future of these civilisations is clearly the great question. Looking across the civilisations it is clear that until the last century, their political systems were totally different. The Chinese had an Imperial-bureaucratic centralised system. After brief experiments during the Republic, it reverted for thirty years to another form of absolutism – Communist Rule. Only within the last thirty years has there been a serious attempt to increase political participation, through the delegation of power to the provinces and autonomous regions.

Japan experimented with democracy after the end of the imperial system in the 1870s, but it also reverted to another form of totalitarian rule under the God Emperor in the 1930s. Then, since 1945, it has formally adopted Western-style Parliamentary democracy. Yet most observers note that underneath the surface there is a very different system, with one-party rule for decades, and a system of cabals and cliques which rule the country.

Europe only began to bring in any semblance of Parliamentary democracy from the middle of the nineteenth century. Though it was often flawed, it lasted for two or three generations before being eliminated in the 1930's. Then for half a generation fascist dictatorships ruled in Italy, Spain, Germany and conquered the rest of Europe. So Europe has only really had a 'democratic' system for a couple of generations. Eastern Europe has only emerged from totalitarian rule in the last twenty-eight years.

In England alone is democracy, of a sort, ancient and continuous. Although the franchise was tiny, there was a balance between Crown and Parliament and the representatives of the middle classes in Parliament were powerful. This system dates back to at least the thirteenth century and became formalised in the seventeenth. The system was taken to America. Yet, there also, the universal franchise only dates back to the 1960s, when black citizens were also included. Many now believe that America is not ruled by the people but by the wealthy – plutocracy.

Democracy

Democracy has two meanings. In the sense that Tocqueville used 'democracy' in his *Democracy in America,* it does not mean the people choosing representatives to Parliament. It ensures that individuals have control over their own lives at the local level – civil society, freedom of association, a sense of empowerment through local bodies, freedom from constraint both of others and material constraints of hunger and disease.

In this broader sense of democracy, there is every hope that as wealth, education and self-confidence increases, this kind of democracy can spread anywhere and even cover something as huge as the 1.4 billion Chinese. This kind of bottom-up democracy is being constructed in China. I have observed it from our first research visit in 2002, where we watched and discussed with villagers the setting up of new village councils. This was a system which was then extended to the cities. We have been impressed by the independence and power of the Chinese regions. This province-level democracy seems to be the way ahead and makes sense when we realize that each of the Chinese provinces is the size of an average nation in the West.

For example the population of Jiangsu province in central China is roughly the same as that of a united Germany, and its total GDP is equivalent to that of Turkey. It obviously makes sense to give it great powers over education, business, transport and culture. This is what is happening. This power is then taken down to each sub unit, so that each township and village or ward in a city is increasingly given the right to elect its own government and officers through secret ballots – though the watchful eyes of the party are still present in a parallel organization of party secretaries.

So there are grounds for echoing G. Lowes Dickinson's observation a hundred years

ago that China in certain ways is the most democratic civilisation in the world – and is becoming ever more so. Lowes Dickinson, a Fellow of King's College Cambridge and the inventor of the term and concept of 'The League of Nations', wrote after a visit to China in 1913.

> *China, so far as I know, is the only country whose civilization has been for centuries, if not always, democratic. There has never been caste in China, there has been, I think, less even of class than in most countries. That equality of opportunity which is the essence of democracy, and which has been denied by every other civilization, has been affirmed by China in theory, and to a great extent in practice, from the date at which her written annals began. There has never been a priestly caste, there has never been a governing caste.*

China could well end up, in the situation Adam Smith imagined with his 'night-watchman' state; the central state almost exclusively dealing with civilisation-level matters – defence, international trade, high-level communication infra-structure.

The situation in Japan is unlikely to change much from the present mixture of pork-barrel central government and a good deal of local autonomy. What will happen in Europe is uncertain. There are dual processes of fragmentation – demands that each 'invented' nation such as Catalonia or Scotland, be given autonomy on the one hand – and an attempt to create a bureaucratic and trading unity with a common currency and union of laws. Whether this Union in its present shape can last with such disparate nations is doubtful – a doubt reinforced when we remember the historical differences of Europe already described and the bitter history of warfare. What hopefully does not seem likely is another European-level war, given the intertwining of nations.

The other aspect of politics concerns the widespread cry for more 'freedom'. That freedom – of speech, action, association, thought – is now asserted to be a 'human right', though people tend to forget that the idea was invented only a little over two centuries ago in the American and French revolutions.

Nor do many people tend to remember that freedom has two meanings – the negative and positive forms of liberty. Negative liberty is the freedom *from* – fear, hunger, oppression of all kinds. It is a legal tradition in England going back to at least the twelfth century, for example in *habeas corpus*, 'I have a body' which is mine and cannot be threatened or imprisoned except after due process.

Once the negative rules of liberty are, it has to be accepted that they entail responsibilities – for we have to be careful and responsible in our treatment of others who also have their negative liberties. The Anglosphere tradition of negative liberty is one which China is rapidly introducing into its laws, reducing the areas where raw power can overwhelm an individual.

The other meaning of liberty, positive liberty, is the right to do things, to say what we like, do what we like, force others if necessary to conform to what we think is best for them, in other words to force others to be 'free'. It is the tradition well represented by the ideas of the 'General Will' in Rousseau and in the seminal ideas in all Communist and Fascist regimes. It is the right of the general body to enforce their views on the individual. This is a tradition which has been regarded with deep suspicion in the Anglosphere.

If the Chinese follow the path of negative liberty, of minimum rights and responsibilities which cannot be violated, then there is a good chance that this, blended with a Confucian tradition which does not have such an idea, except indirectly through the idea of respecting and supporting the other, could lead to a viable political outcome in China. It could move away from the period of the enforcement of a Western-derived Marxist 'positive liberty' within communism, toward something which, although based on a rather bleak view of human nature, has worked for many centuries to protect and encourage the individual.

Bureaucracy

The need for bureaucracy is in direct proportion to the centralization of power within a small elite. At one extreme there are systems where power is in the hands of one individual to such an extent that there is no need for bureaucracy, Weber's 'charismatic' leadership. At the other, there are situations where there is a strong delegation and sub-delegation of power so that the central authorities do not need to pool and process masses of information about their population. They leave it to their subordinates to control the situation.

I saw such a system of delegated power when I first came to work in a Cambridge University Department. I see it still in King's College, where the bureaucracy is still minimal. In both cases, the head of the institution is like a conductor and the central administration conforms to Adam Smith's model of the 'night-watchman' (minimalist) State. Most decisions are taken by people at a lower level. They work as a team on the basis of shared customary laws and precedents, of few but powerful rules, and a great deal of trust. Few things are written down and it is largely an oral, personalized, system of power.

Leadership is about 'character', 'judgement', 'trust' and the 'reasonable man'. It was the system I had learnt as a prefect at my boarding school, and which formed much of the nucleus of the way in which the British Empire was administered by a tiny number of professional administrators.

Such a non-bureaucratic system is the one which Tocqueville marvelled at in England in the early nineteenth century. He contrasted it with the over-blown, written-rules-based, paper-hoarding, surveillance-state of his homeland in France. France, as well as much of continental Europe, is an example of a bureaucratic state which tries to create rules for everything in order to avoid corruption and inequality. There is a centralization of power into the hands of a supposedly professional and independent set of full-time officials, highly trained and 'impartial' and produced by a particular educational system.

While the Continent is one example of this heavy bureaucratic system, perhaps the most extreme, and certainly the longest enduring and largest, is the Chinese bureaucratic

State. After its abolition of sub-delegation of power to a feudal aristocracy over two thousand years ago, the Chinese set up a meritocratic system of Confucian mandarins. China moved inexorably to a Paper Empire, based on endless reports and filing systems, where attempts to standardize the complexities of life and bring them within one system was ever-present. All deviations from this were 'corruption', and the battle against such corruption, in other words the threatened undermining of absolute standards of probity and equity, are an obsession in present China. Yet it is one of the ironies of life that bureaucracy is not a cure for corruption, but perhaps one of its causes.

Geographical mobility

Many 'modern' people live a geographically mobile existence. We are born in one place, educated and trained elsewhere, work and move several more times in our lives, and die far away from our birth place. It is important to remember that the vast majority of our ancestors, until very recently, did not live like this.

Characteristically, in a peasant society, people are born, marry and die within the same community, or small group of villages. A peasant family tries to 'keep the name on the land', that is to maintain the link of family and landholding. The people you know as a child are those who come to your wedding and who will one day bury you. You may move to another village at marriage, especially if you are a woman, but it will not be more than a few miles away.

This pattern is behind strong communities and the multi-level relationships of an enduring kind with people whom one has known for all of one's life. The intertwining of blood relations, a fixed place, and a sentiment of belonging which is the essence of 'Community' is both caused by this pattern and reflected in this geographic immobility.

Such a typical model fits peasant civilisations, including our examples of China and Europe. There are many descriptions of the intense, locally bounded, worlds of peasants. It is this background which makes the huge labour migration from the countryside into the vast cities of China in the last two generations even more extraordinary.

Of course, some people have always moved, and the meritocratic system and love of trading meant that some did move around in traditional China, as they did across Europe. Yet it is still true that the vast majority of lives were lived out within thirty or forty miles of where you were born.

Given this normal feature, it is not surprising that most historians assumed that the same was true of the other two civilisations, Japan and the Anglosphere. For example, R. H. Tawney, one of the leading economic and social historians of his generation, wrote of sixteenth century England that 'most men have never seen more than a hundred separate individuals in the course of their whole lives, where most households live by tilling their great-grandfather's fields with their great-grand-father's plough'.

It was therefore a considerable shock when I studied local records in the English past and found that this immobility was largely a myth. From the earliest detailed records, that is in the thirteenth century, it becomes clear that there was a different situation. Of course some people did not move, for example serfs bound to their masters. Yet, particularly after serfdom faded away from the middle of the fourteenth century, the country dwellers were mostly mobile. Very few of those born in the parish of Earls Colne in southern England which we have studied died in that village.

By the seventeenth century it is estimated that up to a quarter of the population of England had lived in London for part of their life. The normal pattern was to be born in one parish, go to another a few miles away, or to a city, as a servant or apprentice, around the age of eight to twelve. After a further seven or eight years, a person would move to another and perhaps marry. Through the following years they might well move several more times, living in all in half a dozen places before death.

This huge difference between England and the normal 'peasant' pattern is very significant. The English pattern was taken to North America and helps to explain its persistent high geographical mobility to this day. It has many consequences. One of them links us back to the 'enchantment of the world'.

Community and Association

It is very natural to feel that a landscape into which one has been born, and where one's family have lived for generations, has some deeper link to us, invisible to the normal eye. The graves are those of kin, the childhood fantasies are still partly around one, the natural and social world are interblended. There is a world behind the surface of the trees and waters.

The experience of an animistic world which we find recalled in William Wordsworth's poetry, I partly felt as a child growing up in Wordsworth's home valley in the Lake District. It was broken for both Wordsworth and myself when we left, Wordsworth for Cambridge, I for Oxford. I never returned except for holidays, or when I moved, like Wordsworth himself, to another part of the same region.

Japan falls on the Anglosphere side. Although Japanese rural life looked to outsiders as if it was immobile and 'peasant', historical lists of inhabitants, novels and other materials suggest that again many people wandered to other villages or into the densely packed cities which were long a characteristic of Japan.

As in England, the system of inheritance which promised no security in the parent's farm, and ejected all but one possible heir, is one of the factors which lay behind this.

So again we have a split between China and Europe, long filled with largely immobile peasants, and the Anglosphere and Japan, far less attached to birth place and hence lacking real communities.

Familism and Individualism

Another striking feature is the way in which the family is linked to the rest of society. In the case of China, until recently, the clan and family remained the unbroken foundation. The relation of parent to child was the pivot of the political system, and the wider family was the important social, economic, political and ritual unit. All was, ultimately, about family. The sphere for freely interacting, contractual, relations was limited. There was never a break with one's parents. It was a civilisation based on birth-given status, whether in kinship or gender, even though it curiously did not have any kind of caste or hierarchy of classes.

The case of Europe was not as extreme as China, but nevertheless, compared to the Anglosphere, it seems that over much of this area the family is still the foundation. The relation of children to parents, between brothers and sisters, to wider kin, and the gendered opposition of superior males to inferior females, is still widely present through much of Europe. Politics, economics, the professions and culture are suffused with family sentiments and dynamics.

So two of our cases could be described as broadly 'familistic'. Another two civilisations are different to each other and also to the above. The Japanese family is structurally, in terms of naming kin, concepts of whom we are descended from, and inheritance through one child, almost identical to England. Yet while the family forms into small groups and children can easily be shared or adopted, there is a familistic flavour which strikes an English observer as odd.

Japan seems a bit like Highland Scotland, the family seems more important and family sentiments spread out into economic, social and political life more strongly than in much of England. The great businesses and farms, the great family lines, whether in Kabuki or Sumo wrestling or even academic life and the criminal organisations, have echoes, an emotional flavour, which is somehow linked to the family. They feel rather like a monastic order where people are called 'father', 'Mother Superior', 'brothers and sisters', all members of the 'Family of Jesus', even though they are probably not blood relations.

Against all of this the Anglosphere stands out as highly individualistic and almost anti-family. Of course people are born and grow up with parents and keep contact with close relatives. Yet there is no permanent shared resource, for example brothers would not normally be expected to educate their brothers' and sisters' children. There is no common fund and families have no great interest in the marriage of distant relatives. Family gatherings are often infrequent and perfunctory, the family is scattered in space and children can end up at opposite ends of the class system.

What has happened for over a thousand years in England is that the intense bonds, the 'atom of kinship', has been split. The children, either literally or metaphorically, learn to be independent and to go out into Society. Their main interactions, through various institutions and associations, are with strangers, who quickly become friends, colleagues, neighbours, teammates. This is now mainly a world of networks, of 'contractual' (chosen) relations. We now have autonomous individuals who can vote, marry, trade and save, enjoy their leisure, as they individually wish, without great pressure from their family.

Of course this is a simplified picture. Some families, especially where there is a lot of money at stake, are closer than others. Ethnic minorities and some Jewish and other religious groups put a greater emphasis on the family. Yet most people live a life where the family, while very important for the first years up to puberty and a little beyond, recedes as the children leave home, never to return except for 'holidays'. This is an old and unusual pattern, invented on a civilisational scale in England and then taken to America. It is the basis of the modern economy, society and politics, of market, democratic, individual liberties, and of individualism.

The destruction and revival of civilisations

Another pattern which emerges when we look at all the civilisations together is the difference in the way that they have evolved over long periods. Chinese history reminds me of a great tree, growing for thousands of years, but every few hundred years cut right back to a stump just above the ground by some cataclysmic event; the Wars of the Three Kingdoms, the Mongols, Manchus, Opium Wars, Taiping and Boxer rebellions, the Sino-Japanese War and the Communist period.

Each time China appears to be nearly destroyed. Yet half of its structure is underground and soon it puts out small shoots which grow rapidly and vigorously. The same tree grows up again, perhaps with more stems. It does not develop or change much; the Han, Tang, Ming, Qing, two thousand years of history hardly changed the basic culture, laws or language. China is one pattern, continuity, abrupt breaks, then a period of energetic and creative growth, a prime example being what is exploding in China now.

Another pattern is provided by both Japan and Britain. This is of continuous, incremental, and mostly non-revolutionary evolution. Hence the trees start small, put out branches and leaves, and grow into a huge mass. If one wants to understand Britain, one has to work oneself back along various intertwined branches, to the origins of each. Tocqueville used the metaphor of tracing back along winding paths to their source. So Japan and Britain are both unchanged yet constantly changing, looking old or new depending on the way you observe them. They embed ancient laws and traditions alongside newly invented ones.

Europe, like China, is both old, with relics of Greece and Rome. It is also new. It is also continuous, but has suffered terrible catastrophes which have cut it back to its roots. The most dramatic were the Germanic, and later the Mongol invasions. Yet there have also been the ravages of plagues, constant wars, culminating in the devastation of the First and Second World Wars.

So Europe has the deep drama of destruction and revolutions in a way which Britain was spared. Yet, like China, after the greatest of these destructions, five hundred years after the Roman Empire collapsed, Europe came back into vigorous life and flourished between the Twelfth Century Renaissance and the end of the sixteenth century in a way which led into the Renaissance and the Scientific Revolution, laying the basis of much of modern world knowledge.

Then, however, it seems to have experienced an oddly parallel development to China. It reached some kind of ceiling, a high-level equilibrium in all of its institutions, the economy, politics, social structure. So that by the time of the French Revolution it was largely politically absolutist, caste-based, with a declining economy and an ever greater misery amongst much of its peasantry. This was most dramatic, perhaps, in Eastern Europe, with the 'second serfdom' and in Russia. Europe had reached what seemed like a dead end. Finally it found a way out by following the British escape into the industrial use of stored energy and the application of new reliable knowledge.

America was different again, for it was 'born modern'. It took from Britain a balance of powers, limited government, free market, a personal and non-hierarchical religion, legal protection for the individual. It was a young tree of the British kind, without the thousand years of winding and intertwined branches. Hence, as Tocqueville argued, it is relatively easy to understand. It was built on a simple grid – Equality, Liberty, Individualism. This gave it immense vigour as it opened up its huge natural resources, so that it would come to dominate the world for perhaps three quarters of a century.

Our modern world was not predictable or predestined. It was a giant accident and there is no sign whatsoever that modern capitalist, democratic, individualistic and industrial civilisation would ever have developed naturally in China, Japan and continental Europe.

Religion and Philosophy

Buddhism

BUDDHISM WAS FOUNDED by the Buddha in around 520 B.C. Christianity was founded half a millenium later by Jesus. Mohamed started to preach his revelation in 610 A.D. another half millenium after Christ. There is a great deal which they share, though there are also significant differences. We can examine first the nature of the three Revealed Religions and then look at some of their effects.

Some scholars have suggested that Christianity derived its monastic, celibate, male, monastic tradition from Buddhism. This was evident even in small details, such as the shaving of the monk's head, a tonsure, which Christianity copied from Buddhist monasteries. These are the two great monastic religions and their monasteries are a profound source of their strength and success.

In monastic organizations, people are taken out of their families into 'fictitious' families not based on blood, where celibacy is central to stop the family 'corrupting' the institution. Hence the similarity of Oxford and Cambridge Universities until the middle of the nineteenth century (where the Fellows of Colleges were not allowed to marry), and the earlier Benedictine and Cistercian Christian monastic organizations, and those of many Buddhist sects. There is a huge contrast to Hindu, Judaic and Islamic traditions, which keep people within their birth families and encourage universal marriage.

There is a horse-hair, self-denying, asceticism about Buddhism and Christianity. In their extreme form they encourage a withdrawing from the world. In their disapproval of waste, dirt and opulence they seem similar. Of course there is often corruption of this ideal in practice but it is a recurring theme and aspiration.

Buddhism and Christianity both see wealth as God-given, a means, an expression of God's approval perhaps, but not an end. Restraint and poverty are ideals, giving rather than receiving, modesty in all things, the middle way.

There is another feature common to the revealed religions. This is the attention paid to self-discipline. When spiritual power is attained through external religious rituals and the work of priests, the individual believer does not need to pay particular attention to self-discipline. Yet certainly in Buddhism and Christianity, the body becomes an important locus of the struggle towards spiritual progress.

Buddhists are famous for their fasting, their simplicity, their deprivations of the comforts of life. The example of the Buddha himself, who left all his inherited wealth in order to live in extreme simplicity and often discomfort was the ideal. Buddhist clothing, food, accommodation and routines (little sleep, praying in the early hours) is one of extreme self-discipline. There is a strong 'Protestant ethic' in Weber's sense – self-control, hard work, abstinence, avoiding luxury, avoiding waste (of time, money, emotion) in Buddhism as there is in Christianity. The extremer forms of self-mutilation and deprivation are to be found in these two cases. For example, in the Chinese Zen sect of Buddhism which led to Soto Zen in Japan, I recently saw lengthy sutras written by an Abbess after long fasting and in her own blood – cutting her arm and tongue (as her master had done before) to provide the 'ink' for the many yards of her scrolls.

The same is the case in the early Christian church. Saint Simeon Stylites on his pillar for many years, the hermits in their shacks and caverns, the extreme simplicity of the great monastic orders, and then later the simplicity and self-discipline of the Quakers, the Hutterites and others is well-known.

I experienced something akin to this in my own Christian-inspired boarding schools, where the body was chastened, fortified, purified and made a strong vehicle for the spirit. Cleanliness was next to godliness, so was hard living in a school whose motto was based on Sparta. We were exhorted to emulate Christ who attained his final goal through extreme pain in the Garden of Gethsemane and on the Cross.

The Inner Light and the Path

As part of the rejection of the rigid, formulaic, parent-oriented, traditional structures mediated by experts (priests), each of the three religions was based on revelation at a point in time. Each of the founders had an epiphany – the Buddha under a Bo tree, Christ when he realised he was the son of God, Mohammed when he started to have his visions and dreams. Each of them acted as a lightning rod, pulling down Spirit through an inner revelation which challenged the standard teachings around them. Each in their way, like shamans, went out into the wilderness and there heard a deeper voice calling them.

Having received this inner light, their message to their followers was to do the same. Truth comes in a revelation, a light within, which gives a person direct and unmediated access to some other dimension – a spiritual and ideal other world. Although there was a great difference between the Buddha, who did not envisage this otherness as a person, a creator God, as did Christianity and Islam derived from Judaism, the Buddha did see himself as a vehicle. The Buddha, like Christ with his lantern, bringing light into the world, was a person who helped the individual through the difficulties of the world.

These difficulties were pronounced – it was a sense of the pain and suffering in the world which first converted the Buddha; Christ was here to suffer, and through that suffering offer redemption and the overcoming of sin and evil. So both were, to a certain extent, engaged in a battle of the single individual against the snares and pain of the world. Here they differed in degree, if not in kind, with Islam, which does not seem to start with the premise of the original sinful individual who has to be saved or redeemed. A Muslim is born saved and just has to remain so. He or she does not have to be washed and purified from an initial uncleanness.

It is this idea of the inner light that gives Buddhism, Christianity and Islam a rather 'Protestant' or even Quaker flavour. Although each of these 'religions' became more 'worldly' over time as wealth accumulated, there were constant reform movements which sought to return to the earlier vision, to that inner light and the individual conscience. Only the believer and his or her God were ultimately important.

In many of the ancient religions, up to and including Hinduism and to a certain extent Old Testament Judaism, the place of the followers was fixed. In the extreme case of Hindu caste, the individual was fixed within the four-fold Varna system (*Brahmins* - priests; *Kshatriyas* - warriors; *Vaishyas* - agriculturalists and merchants; *Shudras* - labourers), with differences of status or purity, and outside this the Dalits, formerly called Untouchables.

In theory, you could not, through personal effort, move from one to the other. For example, you could not become a Brahmin if you were not born one. It was based on blood, birth or status. The same was true for many of the ancient religions of the traditional world.

What is extraordinary in Revelation Religions is that they are based on individual striving. A single individual can elevate their religious status, become holier, through the achievement of merit in Buddhism, through holy behaviour and the pure life in Christianity, and through similar devotion and behaviour in the five pillars of Islam.

They are all meritocratic religions, encouraging striving and dedication. The believer is in all three a pilgrim, seeker, someone on a path. All three concern a future goal or revelation which one can attain through increasing holiness and through personal effort and discipline. There is no assured salvation or predestined position. The individual can, as in society or economy, rise and fall.

Of course there are huge variations as between and within each of these faiths. For example, the Calvinists in Christianity believe in predestined salvation or damnation. Yet since it is difficult to know whether one is damned or saved, one has to strive hugely in order to prove to oneself (and to others) one's 'elect' status. These are striving, active, creeds.

None of the founders started in a propitious position – a prince embracing austerity, a carpenter's son taking on the might of Rome and the Jewish establishment, a small merchant fighting for his life to preserve and spread his individual insights in a highly volatile world. Yet through dedication, vision, self-belief and modesty, they all achieved a miracle. Their followers were to emulate their example and to climb the holy mountain and finally to attain an inner peace and release in this pain-filled world.

It is not surprising that a number of students of these meritocratic revelations have seen an analogy between this activist tradition and the success of Christianity as the birthplace of industrial capitalism, of Buddhism as the back-bone of the enormous achievement of central Asia and China, and of Islam in holding together for a thousand years the greatest trading empire the world has ever seen, as somehow linked to religion.

Anti-formalism and anti-ritual

The three 'religions' all arose as reactions against over-rigid, formal, authoritarian orthodoxies as they saw it. So they emphasised a return to simplicity, true feeling, independent judgment and equality. They were particularly wary of the constricting power of ritual, that is the special combination of actions and words which take over a person and force them through a set of automatic, repetitive, symbolic actions in a certain direction. A central feature of Buddhism and Christianity when they were first practised was their simplicity and anti-ritualism.

Sacrifices, elaborate ceremonies, arcane rituals performed by a priest, mysterious actions and prayers which the believer did not understand, all were to be put aside. In simple words and simple actions the believer was to turn directly in on themselves and through that inward path to approach the spiritual world.

Of course, as all systems tend to do, as wealth and professional followers built up, rituals of a kind tended to return. The pomp of Rome or the great Buddhist monasteries saw the earlier simplicity overlaid. Yet it has always been a strong feature of these reformations that they eschew ritual as a means of communicating with the divine. This is especially true in the more extreme branches, as in the nonconformist sects of Christianity or the Zen varieties of Buddhism. Purity, simplicity, belief and sincerity rather than the making of sacrifices (animal sacrifices were banned in all three) was the basis of the systems.

The afterlife

The great break in the philosophical systems of the world,

according to Karl Jaspers, was when 'religions' or philosophies arose which were based on a tension between this material, physical, world and another ideal order that exists outside of this temporal universe. So Jaspers drew attention to the 'paradigmatic individuals' who had caused the shifting on the world's philosophical axis or 'axial age'. These were Socrates, Buddha, Confucius and Jesus. Along with Laotse, Zarathustra and some of the great Old Testament thinkers, they formed a new philosophical regime.

It is clear that though they were not alone in this, and all of them drew on earlier ideas, the three revealed religions were based on the revelations, in dreams or other inspiration, of another more perfect order against which a person should measure their life and towards which they should follow the path.

Although the Buddha in his goal of self-extinction in Nirvana was not exactly propagating an idea of Heaven in the Christian sense, Heaven is found in Buddhist writings and especially an art that elaborated strong ideas of heaven and hell, where people would be rewarded or punished for their deeds and misdeeds.

The same was true in Christianity. Again, the founder does not spend much time describing the nature of heaven and hell, yet his followers elaborated on this. They took a few simple remarks, plus the whole of the Old Testament with its expulsion from Eden and the elaboration of the power of Satan, in order to lay out and develop an immense wealth of art and literature on the nature of the devil and hell and the benefits of heaven.

Ethical religions

Coming from a Christian background I had always assumed that one of the central functions of religion was to lay out and enforce an ethical code of correct behaviour, and punishments for incorrect behaviour. In fact, as an anthropologist looking at all the spiritual beliefs and systems across the world and history I now find that this is not true: 'religion' in my tradition has been mainly concerned with ritual, relations with spirit or spirits. Ethics were not really relevant. Even today, Shinto, Taoism and, to a certain extent, Hinduism are little concerned with ethics.

It was only the revealed religions, both the Abrahamic religions derived from the Old Testament and also Buddhism, which placed ethics, good and bad behaviour, at the core of their message. In these cases the believer was to be corrected for morally bad behaviour through divine or spiritual punishment, the loss of God's or the Buddha's approval, with various specified consequences. In the case of the secular systems, Confucianism and Socratic philosophy, the control of ethical behaviour was in this world – the punishment by family, friends, acquaintances or a just ruler through his administrative and judicial activities.

What was specified as ethical was, and is, highly variable. With globalisation we now proclaim certain universal values – 'human rights' they are sometimes called. Yet in practice these are often disregarded, partly because they clash with local cultural values.

The other feature of the overlap of ethics and religion which I had assumed, but is again far from universal, is the fact that in all of our three major cases, the ethical oversight is internalised. They are all very individualistic in that it is the single person who scrutinises his or her thoughts, as well as their behaviour, for signs of deviation from the ethical prescriptions.

Various people have tried to capture the essence of this – Max Weber's 'Protestant ethic', Ruth Benedict's contrast between *shame* cultures (where one only feels bad if others know of one's failure) and *guilt* cultures (when it is God who watches) or David Riesman's *other directed* (like a mirror picking up signals of disapproval of others) and *inner directed* (carrying the moral code within us).

However we portray it, it is clear that Buddhism and Christianity are strongly inward-turned in their ethical systems. Ethics is above all about rules revealed by the founding prophet, who, in some sense, lives on and watches over us to see that we conform.

Missionary and conversion religions

As I learnt my Protestant Christianity I grew up to assume that since my brand of religion was revealed by Christ, and was 'The Way', one of my duties was to spread 'The Good News'. I assumed that, like good education, medicine, law, democracy, it was self-evident that Christianity, through its missionising efforts, should be spread to all peoples. We were right, the unbelievers were wrong, or at least ignorant. So the proselytising at the heart of the spread of European empires across the world from the sixteenth century was basically acceptable, even if it was taken to cruel and extreme forms.

It was only later that I discovered that this, again, is far from universal as a feature of the world religions. Many are 'religions of birth', which one cannot (in theory) join or convert into. Hinduism and Zoroastrianism (Parsees) are prime examples. You are or are not a Hindu, and you can't be converted into the Faith. It is possible to become a Jew by conversion, but difficult or (according to some schools) impossible to leave it. Likewise, in a somewhat different way, Taoism or Shintoism do not proselytize – you can practice their simple rituals, but there are not, as far as I know, Taoist or Shinto missionaries.

A map of the world shows that there are three world 'religions' which have spread far from their birthplace, rippling out across the waters of cultures to absorb and convert. Buddhism was the first, rapidly spreading from southern Nepal and northern India across most of southern and eastern Asia within half a millennium and finally reaching and transforming Japan. Christianity, of course, did the same, and in the chapters in this book on the Euro and Anglo spheres I have outlined how these two religious-based civilisations spread from the Ural Mountains to most of the Americas and far beyond.

In fact, in these turbulent and troubled days, when many of the old certainties seem to be being swept away in the 'post' modern 'post' everything conflict of relative truths and huge economic, social and technological change, the three world missionising ethical religions, Buddhism, Christianity and Islam are flourishing. Contrary to most rationalist beliefs that they would die in the face of science and capitalism, they seem to be undergoing a resurgence.

It is not difficult to see strong examples of this. China is returning to Buddhism. Korea is devoutly Christian. Central America and parts of Africa are converting to evangelical Christianity. Much of the central belt from Nigeria to the 'Stans' are embracing Islam. Yet, as we have seen, under these labels, and with an undoubted resemblance, the actual practices and beliefs are hugely diverse.

United by opposition

There are many sects and fissures in Hinduism and Judaism. Yet there does not seem to be anything as dramatic and fundamental as the way in which the revealed religions, within a few generations of their founding, and as they spread into contrasting civilisations, split into two strongly opposed theological camps. Not only did the two teams trace their history in different ways, but often they came to despise and hate their co-religionists more than mere unbelievers.

Buddhism is perhaps less deeply antagonistic within its sub-divisions. Sectarian killings, of Theravāda monks by Mahāyāna monks are, as far as I know, rare. Yet there was a great split between the original, more traditional branch which remained in India, Sri Lanka and parts of South East Asia, Theravāda, and the more innovatory, looser, Mahāyāna, which spread from Thailand as far as China.

Not content with this major split, as Buddhism moved north it gave rise to further sub-branches. One was on the high Tibetan plateau where it merged into shamanism and became in Tibet and Mongolia, a more ecstatic and sensual form, Vajra or Tantric. Then when it moved into China, the Mahāyāna vision was transformed, merging with Daoism and Confucianism into Chan or Chinese Buddhism, again very different. Parts of this Chinese Buddhism gave rise to the origins of the Zen sects of Japan – Rinzai, Sōtō, Obaku.

What is extraordinary is that when Buddhism reached these further shores of Japan, it was transformed into such a pure, extreme and purged form that in some ways it stopped being Buddhist at all – it was the most, and also the least of the Buddhist legacies. There is a Zen saying, 'If you see the Buddha – kill him!' This originally shocked and puzzled me. What I have learnt as one interpretation of the saying is that in extreme Zen, all the world is illusion, including the Buddha himself. There is nothing except the self – and even that is a trap.

Just as Buddhism was transformed into two great schools, so Christianity started to split into rival and later bloodthirsty alternatives, culminating in the sixteenth to seventeenth centuries Wars of Religion. Millions across Europe died as a result of, what seem to us, minor theological differences.

The first very large split in Christianity (in terms of numbers) was between the Western, Roman church and the Eastern, Constantinople-based Orthodox church. The line between them coincided roughly with that between the area where there had been a deep penetration of the Roman Empire, and its associated laws, family systems and philosophies, and the Eastern, more Slavic and Middle Eastern influenced worlds. Europe was divided in its languages, cultures and religions – with eastern Europe and Russia on one side and Roman Western Europe and Catholic Christianity on the other.

The first split was followed a millennium later by the Reformation and Counter-reformation, which divided basically Germanic north-western from Roman southern and eastern Europe, namely the Protestants and Catholics. The two centuries of battle which succeeded Luther's break with Rome were bloody and cruel and shaped much of the modern world.

The fact that the founder in each case was a charismatic leader whose statements are often elliptical and open to contrary interpretations was one factor. Another was that the tradition was taken on by Apostles, who often started to diverge in their interpretations. Because all three spread to very diverse cultures, in their travels they adapted to local conditions and altered. There are grounds for associating each of the splits to the underlying major differences in geography, family system, and pre-existing religious beliefs of their new homes. So it is perhaps not surprising that there are splits – we might have expected more.

Religion and the family

One consequence of the emphasis on the inner light is the curiously similar, but historically exceptional, anti-familism of the three revelations. Almost all societies are ultimately based on the family and the loyalties and emotions within it – the clan, tribe, lineage, parental authority, arranged marriage. This is pretty universal and is the case in 'embedded' tribal and peasant civilisations from China to the West.

What is curious is that these three philosophies or religions are united in their idea that the individual's primary allegiance is not to blood or marital kin but to a spiritual presence which is larger and greater than the family. It is not the ancestors or family gods that are to be worshipped, but an unrelated Spirit or God.

Christ's injunction to leave one's father and mother and follow Him, very similar to the Buddha's rejection of his family when he set off on his wanderings, is strikingly different from almost all other traditions. And to a large extent it is the same with Islam. The Prophet did not reject his nuclear family, but he rejected many of the primary loyalties of a tribal society.

In each case, there is a strong individualistic streak in these philosophies – the individual decides his or her own life. Parents must give way to their children's decisions, the 'calling' or 'vocation' is stronger than birth ties. It is the movement from 'status' to 'contract', and hence one of the principal accidental origins of modernity.

'Molecular individualism' is a central feature – which comes out very strongly if we contrast each of them with its predecessor – the tribalism before Mohamed, the familistic Judaism based on blood before Christ, Hindu caste and family before the Buddha.

Linked to the anti-familistic tendency, Buddhism and Christianity are the two great religions which depart from this stress on procreation. As we have seen, celibacy is the highest calling. There is no requirement for ancestral rituals to be maintained. The family gives way to the calling of the monastery. So it is noticeable that in both Christian and Buddhist societies marriages are often late and many people, including women, do not marry, though there are huge variations and this is not a universal feature, for instance, orthodox Catholic communities or strict Theravāda communities in Southeast Asia have younger marriage age and most people marry. There is again a strong departure from what went before – Hinduism encourages large families as does Judaism.

Communication in religion

Holy books were to be found in Hinduism and Judaism of course, but, in those cases, they were assemblages of many traditions and many voices. They grew over hundreds of years, a snowball of absorbed ideas and inspiration, often conflicting, part myth and part verifiable truth. This gave the Upanishads and the many books of the Old Testament a different complexion to the single vision, containing all that needs to be known in one statement, of the Buddhist vision, the New Testament and the Quran.

The condensed central revelation in the words of the founder, and it's inscription, meant that writing, and the multiplication of that writing to reach the expanding group of believers, was central. The truths of Hinduism or Judaism were written, yet much of the central belief was passed through word-of-mouth and through inscribing the heritage on the individual by way of complex ritual performances. Much was also preserved by specialised professional priesthoods, the Brahmins and the Rabbis, the keepers of the tradition.

In the case of the three personal revelations, with the break from the birth family, the rejection of intermediaries, the emphasis on the individual believer, much more depended on written tradition and learning that tradition through formal education. The tendency was towards the multiplication of scriptural writings, the copying, and later mechanical reproduction through the printing of the sacred books.

It is therefore not surprising to find that mechanical printing, firstly with wood blocks from the ninth century in China, and then with iron printing presses from the fifteenth century in Europe, grow up and spread very rapidly within two of the three revealed faiths. The earliest complete survival of a dated printed book, from 868 A.D., is the Buddhist Diamond Sutra. Likewise the first major book which was printed using movable metal type was the Gutenberg Bible of 1454 or 1455.

Religion and Education

The sayings of the founding prophet were the source of most spiritual and ethical knowledge. They had to be learned from professional teachers and through books. At the lower levels, unlike Hinduism and many traditional religions, it was essential that young people should be formally taught the elements. This was coupled with a Confucian emphasis on education in China to produce a very high rate of primary literacy across the Buddhist world. There were widespread primary schools of a secular kind, as well as the huge emphasis on the teaching role of the monastic organisations where much of the time was devoted to the chanting and memorising of sacred texts.

People were treated as living books, memorising the sayings of the prophet. This was true also across the Muslim world, with the importance of the madrasas. In each case, the Buddhist monk, the Christian priest and the Islamic teacher was the core of the system and was expected to pass on the vision of the founder in a way which was also found in some forms of Judaism but not in Hinduism.

So education, in the sense of a basic absorbing of earlier truths and a desire that believers should be able to learn the skills to read the holy book for themselves, was often highly stressed – though, of course, there was considerable variation between different branches of each religion.

The way to salvation in both Buddhism and Christianity was through a never-ending voyage of discovery, a path to more profound metaphysical understanding. This being the case, and the need to interpret the world according to the text of the prophet, had another revolutionary educational consequence, namely on higher education

It is no coincidence that just as the oldest printed book was a Buddhist sutra, so the first recorded University in our sense (a place where teachers were assembled primarily to teach a wide range of subjects) was the ancient Buddhist University of Nalanda, founded soon after the Buddha lived in the fifth century B.C. in India, and surviving until the end of the twelfth century A.D. This was the predecessor in Buddhism of many places of learning, and spread from India to China with its famous ancient academies and then on to Japan where, for example, the first 'University' is reputedly Ryukoku University, founded in 1639 by the Jodo Buddhist sect.

This Buddhist University idea may well have been one of the inspirations for the birth of Western, Christian, universities. These, dating from the founding of the first corporate or guild-structured university at Bologna in 1088, and then Paris in 1150 and Oxford in 1167, were deeply associated with Christianity. My university of Cambridge, founded in 1208, was originally largely a monastic organisation – the teachers were ordained, celibate, teachers who were in effect monks, undertaking religious observances every day alongside their teaching. The early Colleges were built on monastic foundations.

The Buddhist monasteries concentrated heavily on the religious texts, with other subjects interspersed. What was unusual about the Western universities was that from the start they stressed other subjects, particular mathematics, logic, rhetoric, languages and sometimes the proto sciences. The rapid growth of knowledge in the world from the first 'scientific revolution' in the West of the thirteenth century, through the second of the sixteenth century, was deeply associated with Christianity and the formative influence of endowed places of learning.

One feature which makes the universities of the Buddhist and Christian kind so powerful was that both regarded knowledge as good, open, and limitless. The prophets had explained that God's revelation was still working, he had set up a <u>way</u> or <u>path</u> and enjoined us to travel it in search of ever deeper knowledge and understanding. The human mind was noble.

Here we may have come across a major difference between the three revelations. The vision of Mohammed was largely complete and sufficient. It was not an ongoing revelation. His followers might add minor amendments, or disagree over interpretations. Yet they would never replace any of his central tenets and to spend too much time and effort in trying to probe further was fruitless – and perhaps dangerous.

Buddhist philosophy it is both vague and complex and the recipe for a never-ending pursuit until there is the final release. It is a vast maze where the traveller pursues an enigmatic genius through their lives. Likewise, the sayings of Jesus are often enigmatic, elliptical, 'I leave it to you to interpret'. The believer takes them, with all the glosses of the Apostles, and the sayings of the mystics, and sets out on an endless voyage. So with Buddhism and Christianity we have open systems, never complete, placing the burden on the individual to act as a pilgrim on the Path to a distant goal.

Religion and Science

Although the individual should be a seeker, a searcher after truth, the Truth he or she was seeking was significantly different in each case. The essence of Buddhism is the concept of illusion, *maya*. We live amidst the confusions and delusions of our senses. The task is to clear this away, to go deeper into ourselves, to shed the illusions and falsehoods until we reach an inner certainty.

We do this not in the hope that we will come to understand the external world, the deeper principles of nature – those laws which we now call 'science' or reliable knowledge. Rather, we should search for the internal laws of thought and feeling, control our own inner being. We cannot change the world through understanding it, but rather through changing our perception of it. Suffering will not be conquered by discovering its roots in abstract laws – disease, poverty, death and their proximate causes. It will be conquered by accepting and rising above them. The Buddha did not set up medical clinics or model farms. He meditated and changed his own attitudes.

So it is not surprising that, despite being the greatest technological civilisation in history by the fourteenth century, it was not in China that modern experimental science was born. Buddhism did not include a creator God who had set down a set of invariable, powerful, yet hidden, laws which, if we are can understand, we can use to change the external world.

For the Buddhist the external world is shifting, filled with contradictions, a kaleidoscope, with no graspable principles. There are no invariant laws, just events, sensations, constellations. There is no God encouraging us to pursue His hidden truths so that we could make His half-finished and evolving world better. Ours is not to change or even understand the world. Our task is to understand ourselves better and hence come to terms with the world.

It has been within Christianity, despite its periodic shutting up of enquiry and distrust of intellectuals, that a unique combination of curiosity, confidence in God's laws, a belief that God was happy for his followers to explore the secondary causes that make our world work, that modern science as we understand it was born. There were many other factors, of course. Among these was the diversity and political fragmentation of Europe, its openness and exchanges with a rapidly expanding overseas world of new phenomena, its university system, its revolutionary new scientific tool, high quality glass, without which modern science could not have developed.

Yet, at a deep level, it seems likely that the Christian position – breaking away from the overly rule-bound Old Testament, yet retaining the deeper lawfulness of the Abrahamic tradition combined with Greek and Roman thought – proved a fertile garden. Some intersection of Greece and Christianity led to Galileo and Newton and to a world which is now the universal legacy of humankind.

Religion and culture

The deep association between cosmologies, metaphysics and artistic systems is everywhere apparent. From simplest societies, with their beauty and elaboration in tribal art, up to the most sophisticated art through the history of the great civilisations, art and religion have been largely two sides of one coin.

We only have to think of the history of art in Buddhist civilisation – the architecture, painting, literature – to see that the Buddha affected every branch of them and shaped the styles and the symbols in untold ways. Whether in the simplest designs and decorations in a peasant village, or the gilded glory of great shrines temples and palaces, Buddhism spread a layer of aesthetic styles across southern and eastern Asia. The colours, shapes, symbols, arrangements, all were deeply influenced by Buddhism, from the extreme reds and golds and magnificence of great temples, to the simple blacks, whites and shadows of Zen.

Much of daily aesthetics was also affected, whether in food and how it was presented, to the elaboration of the archetypal drink of Buddhism, with which it is almost synonymous, namely tea. Buddhism influenced everything from medicines, to family relations, to music and drama, to writing and education. Buddhism was a world cultural style that structured all aspects of life, though its influence varied hugely with different sects and schools.

The same is true of Christianity. Although many now feel they live in a post-Christian and secular age in the West, if we stand back from our world, for instance by consulting friends who are from a non-Christian civilisation like Japan, we are immediately struck by how much Christianity has suffused everything.

It is obvious enough in art – nearly all of the Western tradition of painting and architecture, even after the Renaissance, is steeped in Christianity. It is obvious in philosophy and science, for Newton was only one of the great scientists who saw the pursuit of truth as a religious as well as a scientific quest. It is obvious also in all aspects of education, bureaucracy, law, concepts of the individual.

Christianity is deeply embedded in all of us who live in the Euro and Anglo spheres, in our belief in sin and evil, in good and bad, in every thought and action. Our poetry, drama, novels are explicitly or implicitly shaped by the Christian heritage of the preceding two thousand years. This underlying grammar of thought was then taken and modified across the globe by the European empires.

Enchantment and Ritual

If we skim our eyes quickly across the civilisations something else stands out. This is what we might roughly term the presence of magic, enchantment, the inter-blending of humans and nature, and the way in which this differed.

The Chinese experience is caught by Max Weber when he talks of the 'magical garden' of China. Though this might not be the image immediately conjured up in the minds of westerners who have visited or seen pictures of Shanghai or Beijing, in a strong sense the long trajectory of China can indeed be seen as 'magical'.

Even if you talk to young Chinese now, they usually believe in omens and magical amulets, in astrology and geomancy (*feng shui*), in ghosts and strange creatures in an elaborate folklore. This was even more obvious in China before Mao tried to brush away much of this 'superstition', as he considered it.

You only have to examine the basic tenets of Chinese philosophy and 'religion' to see that much of it is based on an organic idea that man and nature are like *yin* and *yang*, they are deeply interfused. This is absolutely central to what is basically an animistic (nature has 'anima' or spirit) world in Daoism. Yet it is also present in Confucian thought and certainly present in Chinese Buddhist rhetoric. It is certainly the basis of Chinese traditional medicine, which is still very influential.

In China people are ruled by planetary and natural forces which they try to understand and control as far as possible. The winds, waters, earth and mountains are not dead matter, not just neutral atoms, but are infused with 'spirit' or 'power', similar in some ways to electro-magnetism or gravity.

It was such animistic and organic beliefs which the historian Joseph Needham detected in much Chinese thought, and which he believed was one of the main reasons for the absence of a break-through into the dead, mechanical, Science of the West.

Whatever its effects on science and technology, it is a life view in which there is a 'chain of being' where there is no great break between man and the natural world. We are all part of nature, no different from the rocks, stones and trees and animals. 'Disenchantment' in Weber's sense has still not occurred.

It is the same, but perhaps even more extremely so, in Japan. The slight withdrawal into a human-dominated, rational, world represented by Confucius and his followers is less prominent in non-Axial Japan. The *kami*, that is non-human, non-comprehensible, 'natural' forces are everywhere and in everything in Japan. Humans at birth emerge from the earth like plants, then die and return to it. They are not set apart from other living things, or even material objects like computers or buildings. They are not special, they are not the lords of creation, made by a God who gave them absolute dominion over the beasts of the earth. Japan, as I have discovered it to be, is almost fully enchanted.

When we consider Catholic Europe we are in a half-enchanted world. The legacy of Greece, Rome and certain puritanical strands in Christianity, has performed a partial separation. Man stands over and against nature. He has been given dominion over it and was created as a different being. The original unity of man and nature is symbolized by the myth of the Garden of Eden. When Adam and Eve were expelled from Eden, that unity was lost.

Yet certainly when we consider Catholicism, with its belief in miracles, in the wine and bread actually becoming flesh and blood, in holy springs and mountains, in saints and their miracles, we still seem to be in a world (certainly when looked at by its Protestant critics), of magic and enchantment. Only in more extreme movements or people, as in the philosophy of Descartes, do we seem to have moved into an almost purely mechanistic world.

The fourth case, the Anglosphere, is also partly mixed. The Romantic poets, the children's story writers, and some clergymen, still try to preserve the magic. Yet, on the whole, as Keith Thomas has shown in his books *Religion and the Decline of Magic* (1970) and *Man and the Natural World* (1983), the disenchantment largely triumphed. The world, as the poets mourned, is dead matter. The last fairy, Hobbes suggested, was killed by the first cannon ball of the English Civil War in the middle of the seventeenth century. In fact, fairies had probably died long before. If we want to find enchantment in the Anglosphere, we have to visit the Celtic borderlands.

There is a gain in this separation in terms of efficiency and science. Yet also an emotional loss, as many writers and philosophers have pointed out. The effects of these different relations between man and nature in the five civilisations is also currently assuming a new importance as we try to master the huge effects the human species has had on the natural world through ecological (particularly climate) change and the effects of industrialization and over-population.

The different attitudes towards the degree to which man and the rest of nature are bound together also affects much of daily life in another way. If you believe that non-human objects have an inner 'anima' or breath or spirit, then by manipulating them in certain ways, you can change human life. This is the arena of Ritual, that is the manipulation of sounds, movements, objects, for example drumming for rain or taking Holy Communion to bless the crops. Anyone familiar with daily life in the three cases where man and nature are blended, will notice that there are numerous small and larger Rituals to try to manipulate the hidden forces. Even today, and certainly in the past, both China and Japan, as well as Catholic Europe, is full of Ritual.

On the other hand, while the Anglosphere is full of repetitive and standardized communicative behaviour, much
etiquette including formalized greetings and conversations,
it seems on the whole to be largely devoid of Rituals in the
stronger sense. We live alone in a Protestant world where
magic and miracles are diminished, accompanied by our
friends and perhaps with God in our hearts. Yet we do not
attempt to use invisible forces, through the manipulation of
'natural' symbols, to achieve our ends.

Dreams and Nightmares

It is extremely difficult to pierce to the core of a civilisation. One indirect, but powerful, way to do this is to examine the dreams and the nightmares that haunt daily life. The dreams, or ideal types of behaviour to which we should aspire, tell us about the hopes of a civilisation. The anxieties and worries, the way in which this 'Other' mirrors the fears of powers that are believed to be trying to undermine a civilisation's deepest heart and identity, its strongest held beliefs and institutions are equally revealing. Such terrors and dreads, often inherited from previous centuries, still shape the action of people today.

Dreams

The image of the ideal man takes us to the core of a civilisation's aspirations and particularly its system of power. For, in the four examples I have chosen, we are looking at the rulers, the elite who preside over a civilisation and are meant, to a certain extent, to be exemplars for the other 95% of the population

The Sinosphere

For two thousand years China was governed by an administrative meritocracy, trained in the Confucian educational code. The supreme product of this system was the Mandarin. It is therefore not surprising that the qualities which constituted such a person, fitting him into a highly literate and artistic civilisation, are those of the perfect civil servant, the kind of urbane and respected figure who might, in his English equivalent, end up his days, after a top civil service career as a British 'Mandarin', as the Master of an Oxbridge college.

The superior man in Confucian thought, the ideal Mandarin, is expected to show, among other things: an excellent memory, command of the classics, obedience to authority, patience in adversity, loyalty and filial piety. He should have administrative and linguistic ability, mathematical ability. He must be trustworthy, incorruptible and serious. He needs ritual ability, decorum, good sense, analytical logic, passivity, peacefulness and harmony. He should be able to control networks of associates, and have considerable aesthetic and artistic taste.

It is an ideal that is ancient and changes slowly. The ideal type Confucian Mandarin is recognisable from the Tang dynasty in the eighth century, or before. Marco Polo five centuries later would have recognised him from those earlier roots, and another five hundred years later Lord McCartney would have encountered him as he always was.

Below the Emperor, the Mandarins draw together much of the history and culture of China. I now understand better what I have found through China. The widespread gentleness, loyalty and sophistication of most of those I meet, from rural villages up to university professors, mirrors some of these ideals. I see it being taught in the elite schools in China to this day. It is a model which both reflects and permeates the civilisation even after the Cultural Revolution. It provides for all of us a worthy ideal in a troubled world.

The Japanosphere

When we move to Japan we find something very different. The ideals fit perfectly with the feudal past of that island. It is a blend of a brave warrior, with elements of Confucianism, Shintoism and Buddhism to soften the edges. This is the ethics of the ruling group in Japan, just below the high lords or Daimyo. The samurai warrior retainers are what one might call, in Western terms, the upper middle-class.

The ideal of such feudal warriors has been codified in the last hundred years as the 'Way of the Warrior' or *bushi-do*, although the term is largely invented and recent in this use. Yet it does refer to something much older and important in a country where power was delegated down through a military, centralised, feudalism.

The classic synthesis, that made the term '*bushido*' prominent, is in the book by Inizo Nitobe, *Bushido; the Soul of Japan* (1905). A summary of the eight virtues of *bushido* by Nitobe gives us the following: Righteousness, Courage, Benevolence, Respect, Sincerity, Honour, Loyalty, Self-Control. Associated virtues are Filial Piety, Wisdom, Fraternal Respect.

Looking at this set of virtues they seem quite similar to what we shall find in the case of the English gentleman, which is perhaps not surprising since it is acknowledged that the invention of modern *bushido* was partly influenced by the late nineteenth century admiration for the British gentleman.

At first, if we compare this ideal of the samurai with the Chinese Mandarin, we find some strong similarities and overlap – loyalty, respect, righteousness as well as the Confucian virtues of filial piety, wisdom and fraternal respect. Yet we also find more emphasis on military prowess (courage, honour) and less on intellectual and aesthetic virtues, nothing on artistic or literary improvement and nothing directly on the administrative virtues of fairness, memory and discrimination.

One other telling difference is that the samurai has an unbreakable loyalty to his superiors, Daimyo and Emperor. If this cannot be maintained for some reason, he should commit suicide, being worthless. The Mandarin has a more qualified loyalty to the Emperor, which occasionally can be overridden. He may have a duty to 'the Mandate of Heaven' which commands him to stand up against the Emperor.

In the Japanese case, as in the Chinese, the ideal is an old one, which goes back at least a thousand years, and was prominent in its most warlike feudal period in the twelfth and thirteenth centuries.

The Eurosphere

It is not easy to generalize about Europe since there are clearly great differences across time and space in this highly diverse continent. Let us take its most iconic representation, during its most glorious moment (the Renaissance), namely Baldassare Castiglione's *The Book of the Courtier*, published in Venice in 1528 just before his death and published in English in 1561.

When translated into English it influenced the English concept of the gentleman, and hence in turn influenced Japan. It is a suitable book to consider since it reflects much of what is most distinctive of European culture, namely the centralizing, semi-bureaucratic, court environment, urban and urbane.

The courtier in Castiglione's time is not a servant, not subservient and effete, as he often becomes in the eighteenth century court. He is still a lively and highly sophisticated aesthete and adviser, flexible and inventive, worthy to be the associate of Republican governors and great artists. He is the Renaissance Man – cultured yet modest and amusing, the epitome of a high civilisation at its peak. Again we must summarize.

The ideal courtier should have a very good mind, for he is an intellectual who can hold his own with philosophers, great artists, historians and politicians. He should be trained in all of the liberal arts, the classics, the pictorial arts and music, as well as mathematics and geometry.

He should be excellent at presenting himself, an adviser and sometimes a leader who can persuade and charm those around him, making a dazzling first impression by his manners of walking, sitting, smiling, dancing and dressing. His costumes, his voice and skill in rhetoric should sway people to follow him.

Yet the courtier was to be more than a mere minion, a costumed appendage. He should have a warrior spirit, for he might be required to lead armies or defend cities. He should be athletic and trained in the martial arts. He should be humorous, inventive, a support to his patrons, for he was to be a loyal friend and delightful support for the leader.

Part of his charm came from the fact that he was not too arrogant. Although highly proficient and erudite, he should conceal his superiority under a modest cloak. This seems to have been particularly important in a world of potential jealousy and rivalry for power and influence in the court. It also added to the effect of his surprising and dazzling performance.

This is expressed in a quality called *sprezzatura*. This is 'nonchalance', 'careful negligence', 'effortless and easy'. Peter Burke writes that the ideal courtier is someone who 'conceals art, and presents what is done and said as if it was done without effort and virtually without thought'.

This modesty, under-statement, apparently effortless achievement is a curious parallel with the studied understatement and apparent 'amateur' we know as the English gentleman. Yet it may in fact have been partly one of the consequences of Castiliogne's book, coupled with the pressures against 'side' (the word for boasting and showing off used in British public schools) characteristic of small, bounded, ruling classes.

Again we can see it as a long enduring ideal, parts of which we find in the troubadour poetry of courtly love in the thirteenth century, perhaps in turn influenced by Arabic models. The aspirations continue to this day in pockets of our modern world. Some of the top thinkers, artists and politicians of continental Europe still aspire to be Renaissance Men. They have been intensively educated in elite schools and colleges with their heavy emphasis on logic, rhetoric, wit and memory. They still try to be modern day courtiers, Olympian thinkers and creators, suitable to gild the modern courts of Europe, even if these are no longer in Versailles but in Cannes, the Left Bank, Strasbourg and Brussels.

The Anglosphere

The central ideal of the English gentleman is of great interest to many since the phenomenon feels so different from anything many people have experienced. It seems apart from the continental nations, even though it has clearly been influenced by other traditions and in turn influenced them.

Secondly it is such a direct reflection of some of the peculiarities of the Anglosphere. Thirdly it is a personal interest since, as described below, much of my education was an attempt to turn me into a proper 'English gentleman'. So I can write about this from within the system, as a participant as well as an observer

The peculiarity and importance of this curious category has long been apparent to England's nearest neighbours, the French. Hippolyte Taine wrote in the nineteenth century:

> *I have been trying to get a real understanding of that most essential word "a gentleman"; it is constantly occurring and it expresses a whole complex of particularly English ideas. The vital question concerning a man always takes this form: "Is he a gentleman?" And similarly, of a woman "Is she a lady?" ... In France we have not got the word because we have not got the thing, and those three syllables, in their English sense, sum up the whole history of English society.*

He describes some of the radical differences between English gentleman and French *gentilhomme*. He believed that the essential nature of the English gentleman lies in his character.

> *Yet for real judges the essential quality is one of the heart. Speaking of a great nobleman in the diplomatic service, B----told me "He is not a gentleman." … For them a real 'gentleman" is a truly noble man, a man worthy to command, a disinterested man of integrity, capable of exposing, even sacrificing himself for those he leads; not only a man of honour, but a conscientious man, in whom generous instincts have been confirmed by right thinking and who, acting rightly by nature, acts even more rightly from good principles.*

Above all, the English gentleman's central feature concerns character, probity, trust, a certain puritan sincerity and authenticity. In the highly mobile, contractual and individualistic world of the Anglosphere, the ability to trust strangers, to assume honesty, is absolutely central. A 'gentleman's word is his bond'. Without this, you could not have the particular kind of vast global British network of the British Empire, which has been also the foundation of the modern money markets.

Another feature is again the long development of the core model. Chaucer sets out the model in 'The Knight's Tale' in the fifteenth century, describing the model as 'a verray, parfit, gentil knyght.' We find him in Shakespeare. We find him in the upright gentlefolk in Jane Austen, Trollope or Dickens. These were all models I absorbed, ideals of the 'good gentleman' which I was faced with when I went to school in the middle of the 20th century.

These subtle but powerful ideals have attracted attention from all over the world. They are flooding the world with English-style gentleman's educational establishments, which emphasise character as much as brains.

Part of the model's attraction, like any many-sided symbol, is it's very elusive vagueness, flexibility and inbuilt contradictions. It is an education to construct a resilient individual who would be effective and survive wherever you put him down. He might be an amateur, he might be difficult, diffident or buttoned up, he might be something of a grown-up child. He could not compete with his sparkling, artistic, European courtier cousins or with the grave and learned Chinese Mandarins in many respects. Yet he was regarded as someone you could depend on.

Whether such a rare creature will survive in the age of social media and huge international migration we cannot say. Yet alongside his Mandarin, Samurai and Courtier counterparts he stood for a civilisation.

Nightmares

The Sinosphere

China was unified through massive wars and conquests by the Qin Emperor in 221 BC. Since then, given its colossal size, it is not surprising that it has often fallen apart again, with huge and bloody consequences. China's great fear is of social disorder. For centuries the rulers have feared the small spark which, if it catches, can destroy thousands if not millions of lives.

China is so vast and held together by such tenuous force that, as with the famines which historically were present in almost every year in some part of the Empire, there is almost always disaffection and potential rebellion. If this is not suppressed immediately, a small movement can lead to mass eruptions somewhere in this vast realm.

This has been a pattern throughout Chinese history, but let me just confine myself to the period of the Qing Empire from 1644 to 1911. The map at the start of the chapter on China shows some of the major uprisings, partly caused by the expansion of Manchu imperial power, either in the territories of the west, or in creating extra authority over the minorities and the Han population.

In the huge western half of China there were frequent tribal uprisings. Among those noted on the map are the Olot (1750-57), Li (1765), Tarim (1759-60), Hui in Qinghai (1781-84) and Muslim (1825-37). These uprisings and the huge expeditions mounted by the Qing to suppress them and other risings (including the Mongols) need to be understood as the background to current policy. The anxieties with respect to the Mongolian, Muslim and Tibetan provinces, which comprise almost half of Chinese territory, are still there. At any point, it is believed, people could form into a mass secessionist movement which would split off much of the Chinese Empire. Encouragement of such movements by foreign powers adds to the fear.

In the south, centre and east of China, which the Manchus had conquered from the Ming, there are two other major forms of challenge. One is the constant threat, highest in the eighteenth century, of unrest in the vast tribal groups who periodically felt crushed or ignored by Qing rule. Amongst these are the tribal risings in Guangxi in 1790 and risings among the Miao (for instance in 1795-1806 and 1854) and other groups in the southern provinces, including Yunnan, in the 18th century.

These rebellions were often put down by a tactic familiar to the British in their Empire, namely the use of one ethnic group to defeat another. For example the Tuja were used as troops against the Miao and others, just as Uighurs had been used by the Ming to suppress risings in Yunnan much earlier. Nowadays this kind of tribal threat has greatly diminished and the ethnic minorities have autonomous provinces. Yet the war of the Han majority against the large indigenous non-Han is a strong theme in much of Chinese history.

The second type of threat is particularly fascinating and portentous for our times. It is a form of upheaval which is rather unfamiliar to modern Westerners, but bears strong resemblance to the Messianic movements of the mediaeval West.

Such Messianic or Chiliastic movements are characterized by the sudden emergence of a group driven by fanatical religious zeal. Their message gives confidence to thousands and sometimes millions of people who feel that the end of the world as it is presently constructed is at hand. Often a charismatic figure, sometimes in the person of a Christian Messiah, arises. He (and so far it is always a he) tells his followers that they are indestructible and can turn the world upside down. They proclaim that the high will be made low and the poor made high. All the present inequalities and sufferings will be wiped away in the new reign of equality and love. Some believe that the French Revolution had elements of this, just as in the same way the Communist Revolution in Russia, and, more recently, Chairman Mao and Pol Pot with their later Communist revolutions.

Those who believe that the Communist Revolution was yet another such Messianic movement, which succeeded because it occurred at a time of massive disarray in China after the warlord period and the Sino-Japanese war, would point to its costs in human lives. If we add together the deaths in conflict with the after-effects of the attempt to create the perfect kingdom on earth, namely the famines of the Great Leap Forward and the deaths and destruction in the Cultural Revolution, this movement was in some ways the most costly of all.

In the West, where the nearest we have to this is the rise of communist and fascist movements, we need to understand this background if we are to comprehend the apparently heavy-handed, if not (to westerners) paranoid, surveillance and crushing of apparently trivial dissent in China today.

The Chinese know their history and they are particularly wary of apparently innocent, small, spiritual and intellectual movements of dissent. This is why they regard the ritualistic cult of the Falun Gong with such concern and why they appear to their friends in the West to be overly concerned by the threats posed by the Dalai Lama or by Muslims.

The Chinese have been burnt before and when even well-meaning activists, lawyers or academics call for 'freedom' and 'democracy' in more than a subdued way, the menacing specter of China's bloody uprisings enters the minds of the rulers. Without understanding this, the reaction to the protesters who were calling for the downfall of the Communist Party in Tiananmen Square, as well as less dramatic challenges to the State, are difficult to understand. China is so vast that, as the Emperors through the ages discovered, it is either strongly bound together, or can fall to pieces with terrible consequences.

The Japanosphere

What are Japanese fears? Like China, Japan was founded on conquest, but in the Japanese case it was largely through the driving out of the aboriginal peoples of Japan, the Ainu, who now hardly exist. They were killed and expelled.

In the last thousand years there been little threat, external or internal, to Japanese identity or basic political and social structure. There are two exceptions to this before the Second World War. One is the attempted invasions by the

Chinese in the early thirteenth century, which were driven off, largely by the 'Spirit Wind' (*kamikaze*). The second threat was from the arrival of the Portuguese and Dutch in the sixteenth century with their new technologies and particularly their evangelical Christian missionaries.

There was a period in the sixteenth century when powerful leaders, especially in southern Kyushu, espoused Christianity and the Shogunate tolerated it. It seemed that the country might switch its allegiance from a mix of faiths and sects of a Chinese style to a new monotheistic religion – Christianity. Yet within a generation, the Shogunate became suspicious and started to outlaw the religion and in a relatively rapid period of a few years the Christians were defeated.

What happened then is a strong indication of the nature of Japanese culture. Rather than permitting the minority sect to remain, tolerated if contained, the threat was extirpated. The Christians were executed, often crucified. Their property and families were destroyed. All vestiges of Christianity were outlawed. Even activities like bringing in bread and wine, thought to be powerful and secret symbols of the Eucharist, were banned in Japan. So by half a century later, although there were in fact a few secret survivors, the religion was destroyed and the unity of Japan restored. For the next two and a half centuries all contagious and infectious ideas and people were strictly quarantined so that they could not enter Japan.

Nowadays, of course, the situation is different and Christianity has been widely permitted and perhaps one percent of the Japanese population is Christian. Yet the Japanese have something of the nervousness of the Chinese about charismatic Messianic movements, often of a right-wing nature. Most famous is the Doomsday cult, Aum Shinrikyo, which undertook the sarin gas attack on a Japanese subway in 1995.

On the whole, however, the Japanese reaction to 'The Other'

in their midst is special. As long as the infiltrating elements lie dormant and make no fuss, they can be ignored. Thus there are a large number of migrant workers from around the world in Japan. They have no legal position, but are tolerated and widely known about. Likewise, for a long period, the Koreans were in this position, having their own university and parallel organisations but not legally recognised. Or there are the concealed *burakamin* about whom I have written. As long as the surface unity of extreme uniformity can be maintained, and the Japanese identity kept formally pure, alien presence can be accommodated, even if it is strictly cordoned off and given little power.

The Eurosphere

In his book *Europe's Inner Demons* (1975), Norman Cohn outlined much of the detailed content of what has happened in the last thousand years in Europe. This follows on from his earlier *The Pursuit of the Millennium* (1957), which charted many of the European Messianic movements of the medieval period. The nightmares he describes tell us much about the central, usually invisible, core of the Eurosphere.

At the base of the widespread and different phenomena are three intersecting features. The first is that Europe has been for a thousand years a battleground between the three forms of monotheism – Judaism, Christianity and Islam. This war has sometimes been joined by a fourth religious variant, a powerful religion from the East, Manichaeism.

The second force is something I have alluded to. This is that in Europe as a whole, culture and society are united – in order to be French, Spanish, Italian it is not enough to obey the laws and pay your taxes. You have to *believe* and *live* as a Frenchman. A major part of this belief and life is expressed in a religious ideology. Spanish, French or Italian identity is expressed and permeated by Catholicism. Yet this Catholic ideology is always under threat, and hence the Demons.

Somehow linked to this is the difficulty of accepting some groups, sub-communities with different cultures, social structures and ideologies, within the majority culture. Whether they are Jews, gypsies, Protestants, Moorish Muslims or whoever, they grate against the wider cultural mores. Periodically the irritation rises to a peak and there are catastrophic purges and pogroms. Then the various societies settle back again into an uneasy calm. Even when actual enemies within do not seem to be a real threat, they tend to be invented.

Let me very briefly chart the major eruptions of the European nightmare over the last thousand years. The first major threat was the fear that a rival to Christianity had seeded itself in the south of Europe, particularly in southern France. This was a powerful moral and intellectual movement inspired by Oriental beliefs which challenged the biblical orthodoxy. Known as Manichaeism, it is a dualistic religious system with Christian, Gnostic, and pagan elements, started in Persia in the 3rd century by Manes (*circa* 216– *circa* 276) and based on a supposed primeval conflict between light and darkness. It was widespread in the Roman Empire and in Asia, and survived in eastern Turkestan (Xinjiang) until the 13th century.

The beliefs challenged the central dogma of Christianity, namely the belief that God was all-powerful and ruled heaven and earth. Instead, it was argued that the cosmos was split into Good (above) and Evil (ruling this world). The Devil was as powerful on earth as was God in the Heavens. There were many other subsidiary beliefs, but this is the one that challenged the whole Christian message. It gripped the mind of many powerful nobles, mainly in southern Europe and by the twelfth century there was a real chance that Europe would abandon Christianity and become a Manichaean civilisation.

The battle against Manichaeism in Europe reached its climax in the Albigensian or Cathar Crusade (1209–1229) a military campaign initiated by Pope Innocent III against the Albigensians in Languedoc in the south of France. The Cathars were destroyed in a series of hugely violent repressions ordered by the King of France. The first major demon had been exorcised

Yet there were others that lurked in the European imagination. One which returned again and again to haunt Europe were the Jews. Much of European history, from the mediaeval pogroms, through the ghettoization later on, to the frequent expulsions and persecution continued as a sub theme of European history.

This was why Hitler's plan to eliminate the Jews was called 'The Final Solution'. It would for once and all eradicate this alternative to central Christian, 'European', 'Aryan' identity. Hitler's solution, being carried out when I was a young child, destroyed approximately six million Jews in Europe. The events are the most dramatic and recent of the examples of an anti-Semitic theme which deeply infects European culture.

A third was the internal crusade against Islam, lasting almost seven hundred years and only ending in 1492, mainly fought in Spain and Portugal, and towards the end enlisting the support of the Catholic Inquisition. The church and state united to expel the Moorish Muslims, to cleanse Europe of a competing monotheism. Alongside this were a series of bloody crusades from the eleventh century onwards, trying to re-conquer Jerusalem and what were perceived as the original Christian lands.

As well as struggling with real human 'heretics' with explicit alternative beliefs, there was from the fifteenth century another war against a set of demons – the great witchcraft conspiracy. Again, encouraged by the Catholic Church in league with the State, it appeared to be the case that, with the use of judicially sanctioned torture and special legal methods, it was possible to locate a vast conspiracy against European civilisation. Satan, with his thousands of perverted followers forming into a number of underground 'cells' or 'covens', was seeking to overturn Christian decency.

The witches were believed to be killing people and destroying their property, engaging in sexual orgies, eating human flesh and blasphemously subverting sacred Christian rituals such as the Holy Communion. For three centuries these evil people were tried and killed – many tens of thousands of them. Only in the eighteenth century was it finally established that they had never existed at all. They were the 'terrorists' of their age, yet they had been manufactured by the machinery created to counter their supposed conspiracy. They were an imaginary evil, believed in by many of the greatest minds of their age.

Thus the background to European life, a nightmare seen very recently again in the middle of the twentieth century in Germany, is one where threats to the supposed core identity of Catholic Europe are seen as deeply menacing. Having rejected the Manicheans, the Islamic Moors and the witchcraft threat, Europe is now bracing itself, it seems, for yet another round in its war. This time the threat if from a 'flood' of non-Christians from Africa and the Middle East. Let us hope Europe learns from some of its past tragic over-reactions and inventions.

The Anglosphere

While many of the nightmares of China, Japan and Europe are tinged with much ideological, moral and cultural threat, the Anglosphere demons tend to be more one-dimensional. This can be explained by the 'point of origin' of England and America.

In both, the starting point was an expansive war against political neighbours. The Saxons expanded and largely destroyed or subdued the ancient Britons, Celts and other groups on their neighbouring fringes and incorporated their lands into their kingdoms. Their enemies were open and obvious, political rivals with weapons who could be killed or disarmed. So the Scots were finally subdued, as well as the Irish and the Welsh.

Though there were minor outbreaks of anti-Semitism and witchcraft persecutions, they were on a scale and of a nature which is different from the European phenomenon. The main fear was of political subversion, whether of the deposed Stuart King's followers or later of communism and fascism. On the whole, the Protestant settlement and growth of civil society tolerated considerable differences of opinion. In the growing Empire, cultural differences were not seen as a challenge to the core identity of the British on their home island.

America took this rather secularized Protestant view, but soon entered onto a re-run of the conquest period of the Saxons. Their foes were not Scottish or Irish clans, but the tribes and confederations of the indigenous Indians – among them the Sioux, Cheyenne and Crow. Thus began the two hundred years in which there was an almost complete destruction of the original inhabitants of North America, using the gunpowder weapons which gave the settlers their advantage.

So America was born with the spirit of a moving, warring, frontier, with a gun in one hand and a Bible in the other. Behind the advancing guns were the wagons with the whiskey and cheap manufactured goods, the ploughs and the livestock.

For a number of centuries this huge continent was not really menaced by any outside or internal threat except the divisions between the northern settlers and the slave-owning southern states. Only with the advent of planes and rockets and the growing flood of immigrants did America begin to fear the 'Other'.

As in the British case, the threats were largely one-dimensional, threats to political power. Although there were a few witchcraft cases in Salem in the later seventeenth century they were on a tiny scale. The real threat of invisible enemies became 'the reds under the beds', that is to say political conspiracies believed to be threatening 'the American way of life'. The aptly named un-American Activities Committee headed by Senator McCarthy used many of the same methods as the anti-witchcraft movements on the continent – gossip, spying, forcing people to accuse their friends. For a while the Committee unearthed a large conspiracy. Yet, as with the witchcraft fears, when challenged and exposed, the whole paranoid movement collapsed.

Yet its seeds, the fear of political subversion, have not gone away. Perhaps the innocence and lack of experience of such things has made America particularly susceptible to overreaction and panic. For even looking back on recent events, most people agree that the undermining of civil liberties, the use of surveillance and torture, the aptly named 'Patriot Act', rushed through after the attack on the Twin Towers in America, was out of proportion. Yet it is unlikely to be the last such extreme reaction, as can be seen as I write this, listening to a high riding presidential candidate (now President Trump) call for the reintroduction of judicial torture and the banning of all Muslims from entering America.

Paranoid aggression fits neatly into certain elements of the Anglosphere story. It is particularly difficult to counter the self-fulfilling prophecies and extreme reactions since some of the fears, though greatly exaggerated, are well founded. 'Terrorism', a label for anything we strongly fear or disapprove of, is the new nightmare of the Western world. The 'Axis of

Evil' is believed to be 'out to get us'. There is again a titanic war, replacing the brief respite after the long struggle of the 'Cold War'.

One day people will be amazed and saddened by the overblown features of our current 'Wars on Terror'. They will realize that they largely mirror our own anxieties in the West, much of it stemming back a thousand years in the battles of religious ideologies. Certainly, looked at from China, much of it seems puzzling, a war between western interpretations of God's will, a God who the Chinese do not believe exists at all. Yet given the history of Europe and the current atmosphere in our world of instantaneous global communications and rapid movement of large numbers of migrants, we begin to understand some of the West's inner dynamics.

Difference and tolerance

The fear of multi-culturalism

SAMUEL HUNTINGTON'S BOOK is half about the clash between civilisations. What equally concerns him is the battle of civilisations at another level – that is in terms of the inner dynamics or core of each civilisation. The two arguments are inter-twined and succinctly stated as follows.

> *Multiculturalism at home threatens the United States and the West; universalism abroad threatens the West and the world. Both deny the uniqueness of Western culture. The global monoculturalists want to make the world like America. The domestic multiculturalists want to make America like the world. A multicultural America is impossible because a non-Western America is not American. A multi-cultural world is unavoidable, because global empire is impossible. The preservation of the United States and the West requires the renewal of Western identity. The security of the world requires acceptance of global multiculturality.*

Huntington notes that the huge increase in both physical, migration between the world civilisations, and the way in which their ideas, technologies and material cultures now spread so rapidly, means that the core identity of each is threatened by infiltration from outside. This is clearly something which particularly worried him, especially in relation to infiltration from Latin America, his last book was titled *Who Are We? The Challenges to America's National Identity* (2004).

Huntington's prescription, based on the belief that it is not only desirable but possible to keep out 'multiculturalism' is more understandable in the context of the time, because even in the 25 years since he wrote his first article, the world has changed hugely. The flow of people and the flow of information via television and the Internet has risen exponentially. When he wrote it might still have been just about feasible to think of building a wall against the Mexicans. Now it is plainly ridiculous, even if the current President of the United States still plans to try to do so, in the same way as the fences and walls to keep out the migrants from the east and south wanting to enter Europe is just a sticking plaster, giving a sense of, 'doing something about it', some kind of control.

Given what is now happening we need a new approach, which accepts that we can be both multicultural and yet have a core to our civilization and remain unified when necessary. We need to work out how we can both be true to our separate cultural identities and also have loyalty and even affection for our 'civilisation'. These are areas where social anthropology has a great deal to contribute since its particular concern has long been with cultural difference and similarity.

Dealing with difference

Sinosphere

China has tried to deal with difference over its 2200 year history in two main ways. In relation to the surrounding countries, potentially allies or enemies, and certainly different, it has tended to deal with them as tributary states. The neighbouring states and groups can maintain their own systems and differences, but indicate that they are no threat by periodically coming to the Imperial capital to express their junior status and respect for the Emperor. The relationship is also usually underpinned by an exchange of gifts and statements of good-will. It is usually strengthened by some movement of peoples. It is not an Empire in the western sense, conquered and absorbed in some way into China, but a senior brother and junior brother model.

The size of China and the variation within it's huge Empire means that we find a system not dissimilar to certain aspects of the British Empire. For most of Chinese history, the minorities were allowed to maintain their cultural and social differences, but were expected to adhere to the general political laws of China. For many centuries there was considerable autonomy. From the Qing (later seventeenth century) their local chiefs were replaced by Chinese administrators, in the British District Officer manner.

Nowadays the 'autonomous regions' are just that. They are part of China and Chinese language, education, laws extend into them. Yet a good deal of day-to-day control of their internal business is granted to them and their cultural and social traditions are their own business as long as they do not constitute a threat to the centre. When they are thought to have a potential for challenging the dominant ideology and political system, as with the Dalai Lama in Tibet or some of the Muslims in north western China, there is stronger control, but for most of the minorities this is not the case.

With these two tactics, and with the centralized bureaucratic system, an area larger than Europe has been held together for almost all of the two thousand years, since the First Emperor. It is an extraordinary achievement and has many lessons for our global world.

Japanosphere

The Japanese system is completely different. The Japanese have always been great importers of outside ideas and technologies, mainly from China and Korea, but also, recently, from the West. They have managed to take the best out of what came in, improve it and make it feel entirely Japanese and consistent with the rest of their culture. Hence the metaphor of the bamboo which bends, but returns to its former position. They are great survivors under the various cultural *tsunami* which have hit them over the last 1500 years.

On the other hand, in relation to absorbing outside people, they have on the whole adopted a model of internal cohesion which rejects all outsiders as alien and impure. They tend to be kept out, though, of course, there are exceptions. The fact that the Japanese themselves are from many different origins, and hence are a composite and mongrel peoples with great internal diversity across the islands, is mostly ignored. There is a great sense of homogeneity and cultural unity.

Eurosphere

Europe again has two strands. One is that, because of the diversity of small states in Europe since the collapse of the Roman Empire, there has always been great internal migration. The borders have been permeable and each of the states tends to have migrants from its neighbours, and to send out its own to work or marry elsewhere. So, in many ways, as with the ideals of the European Union, it is an open and in some ways welcoming world. Yet the fact that many of these workers, as with the Turks or Portuguese in Germany, who were long thought of as 'Guest' workers, in other words, people who came for a while, but would go 'home', there is another strong tendency.

The best way in which I can describe this is to realize that for many parts of Europe, identity is not just a matter of obeying the laws and paying your taxes, but an existential identity of culture. Until about one hundred and fifty years ago, of course, there were hardly 'nations' in the modern sense in most of Europe. People were Bretons, or Basques or Bavarians rather than French, Spanish or German. There is still something of this today, though a huge effort was made to unify the language and sentiments into the national image from the later nineteenth century.

For various reasons to do with religion, history, and the nature of integration in the pre-nationalist period, there has been, most explicitly in the model of their Empires, the idea that to live within the unity of 'France' or 'Spain', was more than a matter of being part of a political, economic and legal union. It was also cultural. People were to share the education, language, religion, food and customs. They <u>were</u> French or Italian or Spanish. This gave them, wherever they were in the Empire, passports and free access to the motherland, but it also made cultural difference a potential threat.

Much of the problem of the present situation, for example with the north African migrants into France is caused by the clash of these two strands. They are French with their passports, but if they retain too much of their original traditions they are not <u>really</u> French, but guests who, some think, have out-stayed their welcome.

Anglosphere

The Anglosphere pattern is different again. There is one strand which is shown in the British Empire and its successor, the Commonwealth. Here culture and society are firmly separated. The political, legal and economic rules are universal and must be adhered to. The social and cultural differences are a matter of custom and local choice. There was really no other way to proceed for a small nation like Britain when it colonized a huge place like India. It could not convert everyone, so as long as money could be made, 'let sleeping dogs lie'.

The other strand, however, was that the model of class hierarchies was exported, so that the Empire was riven by snobbery, an endless competition for status. The confrontational and argumentative nature of English law and political life was also exported, as in its particular manifestation in the capitalist market.

Lessons of history

Standing back from all this, is it possible to abstract what would appear to be the potentially useful strands of each solution? Can we learn something to help us construct a global model of uniformity with difference? My choice would be as follows.

China's idea of a tributary system seems a reasonable model if you are a superpower. Rather than trying to conquer your neighbours, unfeasible today in any case, you ask them to show you respect and good-will and to help you maximize your economic and cultural co-operation. Much of what we see in the expansion of China today, for example the 'One Belt and One Road' vision, fits with such a long-term, hub-with-satellites model. Of course it has always been part of the Cold War strategies and 'spheres of influence'. Yet it is more explicit and surrounded by ceremonial and formalization and hoped for mutual collaboration and respect in the Chinese case.

In China, a civilisation which, given the slowness and difficulty of communications until recently was in terms of travel times far larger than the whole world today, could be held together efficiently through a hierarchical, integrated, meritocratic system of sub-delegation. A uniformity of rules, including language and education, with delegation down the chain of the decisions which were better made at lower levels, is not a bad model for an integrated world.

Finally, the generally peaceful and respectful treatment of most of the large minorities in China, though the Tibetan and Uighur cases are more difficult, is in many ways more enlightened than that practiced in many other Empires in the past.

Japan's great contribution is its ability to absorb and improve ideas and technologies. Many of the great Chinese and, later, western, inventions, were taken up by the Japanese, who quickly understood their inner spirit, and refined and perfected them, from the tea ceremony and ceramics, to tape recorders and cars. They are superb at design and manufacture and this is a great strength in a world where ideas and things are now being invented and flooding in from around world. Every country needs to learn some of these skills in order to survive.

Europe has two great contributions. One is that its diversity and inheritance has made it arguably the greatest cultural centre in terms of music, art, literature and philosophy that the world has produced. This tradition has and continues to refresh the world. Secondly, The way it has kept its internal borders open and encouraged movement of peoples in search of a better life, as currently exemplified with the European Union and the welcome offered by Germany to migrants from Syria, is an example for us all. With the long tradition of considerable movements, it realizes how mixed up most populations are, and how much migration can benefit the countries which send and those that receive the migrants.

Finally, the Anglosphere and particularly the British Empire, has some positive things to contribute. In some ways it has been modelled on the idea of a club (the Commonwealth), albeit some of the members were not initially given much option about joining. The club has rules which all must observe, certain basic 'human rights' and legal, political and economic ground rules must be observed. Yet as long as the rules of the game are accepted and followed, what people do in their pursuit of the game is up to them. They can wear, eat, worship, as they think best and according to the customs of their tribe.

The fact that an Empire which was often mired in blood, hypocrisy and exploitation, when it collapsed was so rapidly turned into a club (the Commonwealth), where most parts of the Empire agreed to keep the President (the Queen) and to accept many of the rules, is astonishing and unique. It says something for its perceived benefits. Based on the concept of trust and the Trust, it allows for collaboration with difference, not a bad model for a federal world.

Putting these ideas together, we have to imagine a world which will have a unified economy (almost present now that communism has more or less disappeared), a unified technology (already largely present), a unified social system – increasingly the case, and an over-arching political system which both respects lower level entities, nations as they are now called, but which is above them and can iron out their quarrels.

Mixing civilisations: multi-culturalism

Apart from the problem of the respect between civilisations, nowadays an equally great challenge comes from the mixing of civilisations. Most parts of the world are now like crowded forests where many trees are close together and intertwining. Most big cities have all the civilisations represented within them and even in remote villages people from hitherto little understood worlds are entering, either in reality or through the virtual means of communications. How can we think about some of the practical ways in which we can deal with this threat to older identities and the inevitable clashes between expectations and cultures?

Layers of identity

One way is to remind ourselves that none of us have a single identity, but rather we have multiple identities, nested on top of each other in a kind of pyramid structure, becoming larger and larger in their scope but not conflicting. I first noticed this at school when I use to write on my personal property:

Alan Macfarlane,
Junior Dayroom,
Lupton House,
Sedbergh School,
Yorkshire,
England,
Europe,
The World,
The Universe

I belonged to a 'study' or 'dayroom' which contested with other studies and dayrooms in the house. Yet we all united to play for and feel deeply attached to our 'house' against the other six houses in the school. All the houses joined to play for, or cheer on, the school against other schools. All the public schools united in their attitude to other kinds of school, for example what we considered the slightly inferior 'grammar' schools.

Yet ultimately we were British opposed to the Continent, western Europeans opposed to Asians, humans opposed to the Martians we read about in our science fiction magazines. Or as Huntington puts it 'People have levels of identity: a resident of Rome may define himself with varying degrees of intensity as a Roman, an Italian, a Catholic, a Christian, a European, a Westerner.'

This idea, the basis of much of our life, is how all complex organisations tend to work. You are divided by difference at one level, but united at the level above, as in an army or business company. It is, and was, the basis for the largest bureaucratic organization in world history – the Chinese Empire – which through the Confucian education system and Confucian bureaucracy built up from the individual, to the family, to the village, to the county, to the province, to the Empire. A person can be a member of all these levels in different capacities. So this is one of the mechanisms for multiculturalism and it is epitomized by China. This partly solves one major problem with multi-culturalism, for you can be a Nigerian, a West African, an African, a Muslim and an American all at the same time. There is no necessary contradiction.

Clashes between identities

This is a start, yet it is not that simple. There are many ambiguities and contradictions which complicate the idea of 'levels' of identity. It may be that lower-level identities and loyalties are much stronger, and people refuse to forego them in relation to a higher level when there is a conflict between levels. A well-known example is when E. M. Forster was asked, if he had to choose to betray his friends or his country, what would he do. He answered that he hoped he would be brave enough to betray his country and stay true to his friends. He was writing from a time (the 1930's) and a place (Cambridge) where many young and idealistic undergraduates were faced with a similar choice and some of them became famous spies ('the Cambridge spies') whose loyalty to international communism outweighed their loyalty to their own country.

This loyalty to lower levels (or, as we have seen above also to higher levels) is in fact normal. In almost all societies your loyalty to your family, clan and co-villagers outweighs abstract loyalties to a province, county, state or empire. England was exceptional in basing its law on the assumption that people would come into court and give true evidence which might incriminate their friends, neighbours or even family. The more normal situation is shown by China, for at the heart of Confucianism there is the idea that if it comes to a conflict between your loyalty to your lowest level relationship, your father, and your highest level, the Emperor, you should betray the Emperor and pay filial duty to your father.

The English clash is the stuff of school life and many schoolboy novels deal with the problem. When a friend commits an offence, and the teacher asks for the culprit or their friends to 'own up', what should we do? Or if the state asks you to 'inform' on members of your family who are suspected to be criminals, or even potential terrorists, what are you to do? Does abstract citizenship come before the bonds of blood and friendship?

This leads into a further clash, for while I have ended the hierarchy at the highest point on earth – the King, Emperor, President – much of the tension that continues to exist lies in the fact that, certainly in the monotheistic religions, or, as we have seen, the international ideologies such as communism, your highest allegiance is to something beyond the state. If God is at the top, what happens when there is a clash of duties between God and the ruler? This was answered by Jesus – 'render unto Caesar that which is Caesar's, and unto God that which is God's'. This is a start – pay your taxes, obey the secular laws, but also 'follow me'. Yet quite soon questions of conscience come in, which in Jesus' case ended with his death.

This was particularly apparent to those who were invaded by Western religions, for example to the Japanese and Chinese when the missionaries arrived. These missionaries bought a monotheistic God who demanded a person's ultimate loyalty. This is a particular worry for many people in relation to Islam.

The Protestant movements in Christianity were centrally

concerned with trying to make a split between private belief, conscience and public acceptance of the secular power. Yet even there, from very early on, there were clashes – in the seventeenth century when Quakers, Baptists and others were imprisoned for not showing sufficient loyalty to the Crown.

Play and games

Another way to think about diversity combined with integration is to consider the separation between the rules which bind us (political, economic and social) which have to be agreed upon and uniform, and the rules concerning expression and communication (culture, style, language, beliefs) which are highly variable and a matter of individual choice.

Such a distinction was essential in huge and diverse Empires. Now, when somewhere like Britain or the United States is an internal empire of diversity, it is essential too. It's nature comes out when we compare it to its opposite – Japan and parts of continental Europe – where culture and society have traditionally been merged and hence uniformity of social and culture are essential. This distinction, in fact, has been present in England long before the Empire and can be seen in the title of the first great Law Tract of the thirteenth century, 'On the Laws and Customs of England' by Henry de Bracton. Law has to be uniform, customs can be variable.

The continental European solution is one where culture (what you believe, wear, eat, drink, speak) and society (politics, economics, social relations) are merged. As in the French case, it is possible to turn anyone into a French man or woman but only if they adopt the whole French cultural-social package and *become* French. Religion, education, language, styles all are part of what is needed to be fully accepted.

In the Anglosphere, at least in theory, the highly atomistic, contractual and individualistic system allows for similarity and difference. The rules of politics, society, law, economics, are enforced uniformly across the civilisation. People must pay their taxes, obey the laws and accept the political system. Some basic tenets are not negotiable – individual rights, equalities, freedoms. Yet beyond that, as long as people play by the rules, their culture is their own affair.

This distinction was the basis for the success of the British Empire in the past and the general success of multicultural Britain today. It was less familiar in Continental Europe or Japan, as we have seen, and Huntington recognizes this in passing when he writes 'The French, however, are more culturist than racist in any strict sense. They have accepted black Africans who speak perfect French in their legislature but they do not accept Muslim girls who wear headscarves in their schools.'

It is familiar to China because of its huge size and ethnic and cultural diversity. It has always faced the problem of dealing with people with different languages, cultures and customs over its vast territories. So the first Qin Emperor unified the administration and laws, the weights and measures, the communications and the written Mandarin language. Yet the everyday life of thousands of sub-communities, some of them as big as a western nation state, are left largely to themselves in their dialect, customs and culture, as long as they abide by the universal rules of power and accept the ultimate rule of the Emperor.

This distinction between the rules and the content of so-cio-cultural life, which has worked pretty well for the two largest Empires the world has known, China and Britain, could work, and has to a large extent worked, in the United States. Investigation of a city like New York or San Francisco would show that it is both a melting pot – in terms of rules of the game – and also not a real melting pot in terms of the subgroups of Italians, Greeks, Nepalis, who maintain their own worlds and customs, yet are also 'Americans' at a certain level.

Yet there are serious ambiguities here. It is obvious that there are constant borderline cases. There are many examples, particularly in the treatment of women. For example, if it is your custom to practice foot-binding and breaking of girl's feet, or the immolation of widows (*suttee*), or keeping women locked away (*harem*) or female genital mutilation, is this a matter which is cultural or social and should it be allowed? In these extreme cases, it may not be too difficult to drop cultural relativism and to appeal to universal standards. Yet it is not difficult to find much greyer areas.

For example, what about arranged marriage, or polygamy, or (to some people provocative) religious parades, or certain forms of eating and killing of animals, or clothing in public places? As we face the increasing mix of cultures and traditions, such borderline cases become ever more common and the wonder is how well, on the whole, people have adapted to them – even, in Britain, to the allowing of Sikhs to carry ritual daggers or wear turbans instead of crash helmets on motorbikes. Yet it is good to be reminded that the distinction between social rules and cultural styles is not watertight. Who the bride marries (society) and what she wears (culture) are really interconnected in practice.

The re-invention of the past

A third strategy which has softened the edges of the contact of peoples lies in the area of memory and the re-writing of the past. For many thousands of years civilisations and smaller groups have not been separated from each other. There has been a huge movement of people, ideas and things along roads, seas, through the mountains and forests, and nowadays over electronic communications. 'Purity' of race or nation is a fiction, imagined, invented, to make us close or distant from others. There is no such thing as a 'pure' American. Nor can you have a 'pure' Japanese, as we have seen, or a 'pure' Han Chinese (my Chinese 'Han' friends all have Manchu, Mongol or ethnic minority ancestors).

As for the British, we are one of the most hybrid of all. In my own case, I have only recently discovered that I am not the Englishman (Anglo-Saxon) or Scotsman I thought I was for most of my life. Investigating my ancestors in detail I find I am also Welsh, Scandinavian, German, Dutch, Portuguese, and perhaps with a touch of Indian, Burmese and Jamaican to add to the mixture.

This hybridity is not just one of race, but also of all our cultural characteristics and is one of the reasons why David Hume commented that there was no such thing as a national character in England; 'We may often remark on the wonderful mixture of manners and characters in the same nation... and in this particular the English are the most remarkable of any people that perhaps ever were in the world'. Hence 'the English, of any people in the universe, have the least of a national character; unless this very singularity may appear to pass for such'.

The self-delusion of 'purity' is shown by the anthropologist Ralph Linton. Linton wrote as follows.

> There is probably no culture extant to-day which owes more than 10 per cent of its total elements to inventions made by members of its own society. Because we live in a period of rapid inventions we are apt to think of our own culture as largely self-created, but the role which diffusion has played in its growth may be brought home to us if we consider the beginning of the average man's day...
> Our solid American citizen awakens in a bed built on a pattern which originated in the Near East but which was modified in Northern Europe before it was transmitted to America. He throws back covers

made from cotton, domesticated in India, or linen, domesticated in
the Near East. He slips into his moccasins, invented by the Indians of
the Eastern woodlands, and goes to the bathroom, whose fixtures are a
mixture of European and American inventions, both of recent date. He
takes off his pajamas, a garment invented in India, and washes with
soap invented by the ancient Gauls. He then shaves, a masochistic rite
which seems to have been derived from either Sumer or ancient Egypt.
As he absorbs the accounts of foreign troubles he will, if he is a good con-
servative citizen, thank a Hebrew deity in an Indo-European language
that he is 100 percent American.

Americans, like all other civilisations, including English or
Scots, are a 'fiction', as Daniel Defoe put it – we are all mongrels
and mixes, bricolages and bundles. Our imagined communities are invented and constructed to make life tolerable and
bear little relation to real 'facts'. It is important to realize this
before we essentialize our differences, which leads to a ghetto
mentality, a need to wall and fence and repel the threatening
'Other' who is, in fact, probably a distant cousin of some kind.

So how do we do this – cover over the trails which lead
us to ourselves, learning the 'Art of Forgetting', which Ernest
Renan claimed was the secret of building a nation. Basically
it is about suppressing some memories, re-inventing forgotten
traditions, inventing commonalities. Part of this is what anthropologists call 'structural amnesia'. This is something which
a rich and plural society like America can do again and again,
as Tocqueville long ago predicted. Many analysts have shown
that our idea of 'America' or 'Britain' or 'France' is a recent
invention. Diverse roots, ancient differences and uncomfortable past events are forgotten, and a mythical genealogy is built
up uniting people. This helps absorption, for though large
numbers of immigrants may maintain their cultural plurality,
they may also very quickly readjust their past to fit their
present. So they become British or American, as incoming
groups have done over the centuries.

What the histories show is the ability of civilisations to change rapidly while pretending that they have not changed. Part of this is through the mechanism of 'The Invention of Tradition', which is happening, for example, on a vast scale in China, where pre-communist customs and traditions are being re-deployed. They are often partly invented, though on the basis of something that was there before. Japan and England as islands which were constantly importing their best ideas from elsewhere were particularly good at making alien things seem as if they were part of an ancient, local, tradition.

Liberty and tolerance

When people from different civilisations, or even from other cultures within a civilisation (Hungarians and Spanish, or even Scottish and English) inter-act, there are numerous potential clashes on the border of what liberty each individual has to pursue their own cultural norms. The question of the limits of liberty were partially addressed by John Stuart Mill's suggestion that we are free to do anything we like, as long as it does not infringe another's freedom. If we examine this, however, we realise that it does not get us very far. It gives Robinson Crusoe on his island absolute freedom before Man Friday turns up, but almost everything the rest of us do (or don't do) in some way or other impacts on others.

The endless quarrels, between neighbours, within the family, in business, provide numerous examples. Drinking, smoking, what we wear, how we speak, quickly take us into contested areas where I may want to smoke, get drunk, be naked, or utter racist or traitorous words, but this impacts on others.

Absolute freedom comes at a cost, as the case of the cartoons published by *Charlie Hebdo* and their bloody aftermath shows. That incident also reminds us that freedom is really very circumscribed and is not absolute at all. If the extreme cartoons had been directed against certain others, Blacks, Jews, cripples, homosexuals, the French State, they would have led to an enormous outcry and an immediate ban. Only because they were directed at an approved target, one of the monotheistic religions in France (but not Judaism), were they permitted. How can this conflict be resolved beyond a mechanistic cost-benefit, utilitarian, calculus? Particularly difficult in relation to Mill's formulation is control of the self. Suicide, over-eating leading to serious obesity, drug abuse, serious sado-masochism, watching child-pornography and other private behaviour is not purely personal but affects others. When we add in the harm we do to the general environment, pollution and degradation, and to animals and plants, it becomes an almost impossible tangle of contested liberties.

A related minefield concerns tolerance and intolerance. We start with the premise of tolerating others, their actions and their words. I disagree or even hate what you say, but I will defend to the death your right to say it. Yet there soon comes a point that tolerating what we consider intolerance becomes impossible. Our own tolerance has to turn to intolerance to preserve itself. An extreme form is if someone threatens to kill you. If you tolerate and do not resist, as a pacifist, your own tolerance is extinguished and intolerance triumphs in your death.

So there must be situations where you become intolerant in order to preserve wider tolerance – intolerant of rape, murder, drug dealing, in order to preserve 'our' freedoms. Again, the lines and interpretation shift in the sand when applied at the international level. Can we tolerate North Korea having a hydrogen bomb, or the Islamic state wanting to establish sharia law and a caliphate? Can we tolerate the international arms or drug or people-trafficking trades?

Positive and negative liberty

Another grey area lies in relation to positive and negative rules of freedom. Many have found inspiration in the distinction made so clearly by Isaiah Berlin in his 'Two concepts of liberty' essay, between positive liberty, the right to do something, and negative liberty, the right to be free from something.

The positive liberty tradition is found in absolutist political systems, expressed for example by Rousseau in his idea that we must surrender ourselves entirely to 'The General Will', and hence descending into Communism and Fascism. In this formulation, the State has the right to 'force you to be free' in the interests of 'The General Good'.

This theory is anathema to the Anglosphere tradition, represented in different ways in Hobbes's idea that ultimately we have the right to resist Leviathan, or John Locke's contractual system where non-performance of the contract by the rulers or parents permits us to rebel. It is also found in Confucianism, where an individual can, if they feel that the Emperor has gone wrong, withdraw their consent and loyalty because he has lost the 'Mandate of Heaven'.

As I have suggested, this distinction between negative and positive rules is enormously helpful in describing the mechanisms behind many British institutions – games, the club, fellowship and civil society in general. 'Don't walk on the grass', 'Don't leave litter around', 'Don't carry loud music devices around the grounds', such rules are enough to deal with the thousands of tourists who enter King's College, Cambridge.

Unfortunately, however, the line between negative and positive is not absolute. Take the example of the game of football. There are some negative rules – you cannot handle the ball unless you are the goalkeeper. You can't push or kick another player. You must not be 'offside' (there must be at least one player as well as the goalkeeper between you and the opposition goal before you receive the ball). You can't continue to play if the ball goes off the pitch. That would seem to be about it.

When, however, we examine a game, we find that it would soon end if there were not some positive rules as well. You should try to score goals, you should try to put the interests of the team before your own, you should be as fit as possible, you should try as hard as possible, you should be as polite as possible to your opponents.

The mix becomes particularly tricky in the grey borderland of 'cheating'. You should try as hard as possible to win, but must not do so by using unfair means, such as banned substances, or trying to bribe the opponents, or breaking the rules when you know the referee cannot see you. You should play within the *spirit* of the rules of sportsmanship, as well as the actual rules.

Very soon what starts as an 'external' game with a set of simple negative rules becomes a whole test of character, motives, attitudes and intentions. This is what I learnt in my games-obsessed childhood – 'play up, play up and play the game' is about much more than the game itself. This is why games are a model for the whole of life – for the same is true of economic, political, religious or family 'games'.

Ambiguities and clashes in the law

In much of social life we are guided by rules or laws – don't do that, do this, if you do this the consequences will be the following. In fact all legal systems can only set up a very crude, external, structure to guide life and most of social life falls between the scaffolding. For example, you can have a rule that you should not scatter litter in a public place, but what is litter? Is a degradable thing like apple peal, or spit, or cigarette ash, litter? And what is a public place? Is the front garden of your house where you deposit a mass of stinking garbage, 'private' or 'public'?

This problem can be multiplied a million times as is amusingly shown in A.P Herbert's books, for example several of the stories in *Uncommon Law* (1935). If a road is temporarily flooded and a boat meets a car, should they abide by the rules of the land, whereby you drive on the left in England, or the rules of water, where you drive on the right? Or if you throw snails out of your garden and into your neighbour's are you within the law? The law allows you to eject wild animals from your garden, but is a snail fully wild or partly domesticated by living in your garden?

Another type of problem comes up in the clash between the letter of the law and the spirit of the law. Laws are a first stab at promoting legality, but in practice can easily betray the spirit of the system by promoting injustice. You may be legally entitled in the United States to shoot someone if you believe them to be acting with malicious intent, but is it just to do so? You may be legally entitled to evict an elderly lady from her house when you discover that she has lost her title deeds. Yet is it just? You may be legally entitled to refuse to repay a large sum of money borrowed from a friend because you never signed and witnessed a contract. Yet in every case, while the formal law may be on your side, there may be strong grounds for believing that the spirit behind the laws, which is believed by many to be the promotion of a 'fair', just, and equitable set of relations between people, is being undermined.

This distinction between law and justice is formally recognised in English law in the ancient tradition of having two equal branches of the law, that is Common Law and Equity.

The Common Law upheld the laws of the land, derived from statutes and precedents, and half the business of law took place in Common Law courts. Yet stemming from the King's Court (*Curia Regis*), from at least the eleventh century, and then formalized into a separate court a couple of centuries later, there grew up, under the protection and direction of the Lord Chancellor, the equally important courts which used very different procedures and were based on the concept of fairness and equity. Particularly the court of Chancery, but also those for poorer people, for example the Court of Requests, administered a much more informal and common sense and equitable jurisdiction.

Here people who had lost their deeds, who had never signed a contract, who were poor, women, children without strong rights in Common Law could petition the Lord Chancellor for justice. He could then take extensive soundings, commissions, investigations, to establish the context and implicit understandings, the history and the relationships behind a dispute. If it was found that though the deed was missing, the contract was only verbal, the understanding was only informal, nevertheless it was reasonable to maintain it in terms of fairness you would be supported. If weaker and unprotected people were not getting justice in the face of superior power, the Lord Chancellor could go beyond the Law and deliver Justice.

Although Chancery and other equity courts were abolished as a separate system in the later nineteenth century their practice was retained and incorporated into other parts of the legal system. So formal rules are not everything. Particularly important was the protection which the Lord Chancellor gave to the central device of the Trusts. Trusts could not depend on the Common Law, but on agreed understandings, on faith and trust, which could be protected by Equity.

The lesson from all of this is that alongside all systems of simple rules which guide our lives, there are infinite customs, cultural constraints, implicit understandings, which shape the way in which the rules work. Much of this is never analyzed and made formal and hence many of the clashes of cultures occur because people are working to different, if parallel, sets of expectations.

One of the most brilliant explorations of this is in E. M. Forster's *Passage to India* where the mis-understandings of the English and the Indians are delicately dissected. Another is in many of William Shakespeare's plays. For example, the way in which the 'pound of flesh' in the *Merchant of Venice* is interpreted by the judge in a way which was legally enforceable, but Shylock could see (as could the audience) was in fact not in the spirit of that phrase, in other words a kind of legal cheating. Most of the hugely popular operettas by Gilbert and Sullivan revolve around legal contradictions and ambiguities, from *The Pirates of Penzance* and *Iolanthe* to *The Mikado* and *The Gondoliers*.

What now?

The Clash or Harmony of Civilisations

THIS HAS BEEN a journey of exploration and re-exploration, an adventure through the worlds I have known in four civilizations. I will end by briefly drawing out a few of the implications.

We are faced with an unprecedented situation. The flow of people over our planet is turning from a trickle to a flood. The speed of communications of ideas, attitudes and objects is also increasing exponentially. New technologies, from weapons to medicine, from computing to consumption, are also changing at a breathtaking rate. This is just the start. The world in 2018 is hugely different from that which I inhabited twenty years ago in 1996. That in turn seems light-years away from the world of my school days in 1956. Imagine a future as this pace, of population, technology and social and political change, escalates. What will 2036 or 2056 be like?

In these brief vignettes of four of the most influential world civilisations I have tried to give a rough, preliminary, map. With this, we may be able to make more sense of the confusing intermixture and confrontations of civilisations.

Obviously the appearance of each country is mixed, and there are no 'pure' cases of civilisations. Yet I still believe that like trees or people, each civilisation has certain recognisable characteristics, which is carried on through the centuries. Civilisations are persistent and tough and can last for many generations, even though they are constantly evolving and changing, like a language or a growing tree. Much of their character is laid down in the form of a seed very early, and then this expands and incorporates new elements, but the structure remains largely unchanged. The China of 2022 B.C.

or the Islam of 700 A.D. or the England of the same date can still be seen in many of its aspects to this day.

One way to envisage each of them is through the metaphor of trees. If we think of civilisations thus, and choose a tree for each civilisation, then the five civilisations can be seen as following. China is like the national tree, the gingko. The gingko is a 'living fossil', immensely tough, having survived many thousands of years since the age of the dinosaurs. It has an extremely simple leaf structure, but very powerful and tenacious propagating system (through both seeds and aerial roots). It is a mixture of very old and very new features. It is a miracle of nature, and its ancient and durable character well represents China.

In essence, China is a simple structure, despite its vast size. It has two main constituents. One is that everything is relational, structural, each segment consists of a relation between A and B, as with Yin and Yang. So it is infinitely extensible and practically indestructible. The second feature is that whenever it reforms itself after the periodic massive upheavals of invasion or revolution, it returns to the highly centralised, hierarchical, based-on-meritocratic-training which the Qin Emperor instigated. This unites every person through links up to the top, and through a shared written language and Han identity, it has a sense of imagined community over a vast area.

The Japanese are like the bamboo (which is in fact a form of grass, just as a gingko is a form of fern). Again, very strong and enduring, bending with the wind but almost impossible to break. Part of the reasons for its success is again its system of propagation – through rhizomes or roots that form under the ground so that each new bamboo sprouts from another root, forming an intertwined mass, like Japanese society.

Japan is even simpler in its basic structure than China, and indeed can be said, like the fermented bean shoots in *natto*, to have no real structure at all. It is again all about relations, two hands clapping and the sound they produce, the merging of opposites, the downplaying of the individual. It is a largely undifferentiated mass, both unequal in each relation, yet relatively equal in its absence of fixed castes and classes. There are no hard separations. This world and any other world overlap and merge, the economy and polity and ideology and society are undifferentiated at a deep level. It is neither pre-modern, modern or post-modern, but unique as a civilisation. Again it has a strong sense of common identity and imagined community and a great ability to withstand external shocks.

The Eurosphere can be represented by one of the most widespread of trees, which flourishes both in the Mediterranean and further north, the sweet or Spanish chestnut. Prickly and menacing on the outside, once it is opened it is filled with nutritious nuts which are known as the 'bread of the poor'.

The Eurosphere stretches from western Russia, through central and western Europe as far as South America. It is more complex than the other civilisations for it has two deep notes or points of origin. It is two streams joined and constantly in tension with each other. One is derived from Greece, through the medieval feudalism of the millennium after the fall of Rome. It culminated in the Italian city states and the Renaissance and survives to this day in democratic movements which have kept the medieval separation of the four powers of ideology, wealth, power and society.

The other stream is from the ancient absolutisms of early

Empires, through late Roman imperialism, by way of a revival of Roman Law and the pact between the Christian Church and the Rulers. This strand is centralised, hierarchical, caste-like, mixing religion and politics, tending towards totalitarianism. These two streams have been dominant in different periods.

The Anglosphere can be represented by the British national tree, the oak. Very long-living, tough, used in cathedrals and in the ships that kept England free, but also allowed the exploitation of others and the building up of the largest Empire in history. Complex long-lived, specimens of the oak, tell a story of an old and continuous development, sometimes going back over a thousand years.

This system started on a small peripheral island off Europe, derived from the Anglo-Saxons. It would not be of much interest if it had not been spread through Empire and by the force of industrialisation. As a consequence it laid down much of the dominant language, laws, political system and economic organisation of the modern world.

It is a system which was early 'modern' in the sense of destroying solidary groupings, the family, castes, all birth-given and usually dominating institutions. The individual holds the whole civilisation within him, or her, self and is the only intersection of economy, society, polity and ideology. It is a civilisation noted for its loneliness, confrontational habits, positivism and duplicity. Yet it can also show tolerance, the ability to absorb, a respect for rights and an attachment to humour and playfulness.

So we have these customary arrangements or assemblages of features, which each has its own distinctive 'deep note', yet also influences others all the time, especially over the last half millennium. As could be expected, each answer to the question of how to lead a reasonable and meaningful life brings its members great benefits, but also difficulties. The civilisations cannot be merged, for then, like mixing colours, we will just end up with a dull brown.

Returning to trees, there is no point in trying to force one tree to be another. What needs to happen is to allow them to coexist. Yet if one becomes diseased and weak, or becomes too strong and overshadows the others, the minimalist forester may need to bind up, or prop it up a bit, or cut-off an offending branch that is severely damaging another tree. Yet basically it is left alone to be the tree it is. So the world as a lightly managed forest is a reasonable model of coexistence.

In principle, although the civilisational structures I have described are hugely different, there is no reason why the five civilisations cannot coexist like trees in a garden, once they recognise and understand each other's strengths and weaknesses.

Some will say that this is a romantic vision. That 'history' shows that we are vicious predators. Yet 'history' is largely still assumed to be Western history. Chinese and Japanese history tells us different things. We find long periods, hundreds of years, of peace and reasonable prosperity. Even if we accept that the past has been characterised by vicious predation, we also know that unless we follow the trees, we will all shortly be dead. The self-fulfilling philosophy of the 'clash of civilisations' will destroy us all.

A second metaphor is also useful because it helps us to think about how we can remain different, with our own identities, yet also live together, stressing our commonality and friendship. The metaphor of harmony, which I picture as musical harmony, where, though different instruments or voices maintain their own melodies, yet all of them fit together into something tuneful and mutually enriching, seems a good one.

The essence of harmony is that there is a tension between separate elements, which maintain their difference and identity, yet work together. What keeps the unity are the two rules on which all players must be agreed – otherwise there is discord. One is the spacing between the instruments on an agreed vertical scale, so they have to play on that scale. Playing or singing off the scale is discordant. The second is in terms of rhythm and tempo, so that the players come in at the right moment and for the right duration.

With these two 'rules' in place, the tones and sounds of each civilisation may be very different and indeed it is the very difference which makes for the richness. Societies are, and have long been, based on this idea of harmony, for example in the caste system where each caste plays its part, or in the division of labour and class in capitalist societies. So there are no *a priori* grounds for believing that higher level entities, that is a number of civilisations within one world, cannot do this.

It is not conceivable that we will be able to eradicate tensions and misunderstandings. Even between people who love each other and have come to understand the other over many years there are moments of anger and misunderstanding. How much more so between the huge confusion of fast amalgamating civilisations.

Yet we can mitigate some of the effects through understanding each other a little better and even learn to love each other a little, or at least to admire and be amused by each other. That is my hope, and one of the main reasons why I have tried to understand these five civilisations. Fear and ignorance, at least, can be decreased, and a world in which we are going to have to live for centuries to come, in a set of relations which are unprecedented in history, may be made a little more harmonious.

Books and articles referred to in the text

Anderson, Benedict, *Imagined Communities* (1983)

Bennett, James C., An Anglosphere Primer, http://explorers-foundation.org/archive/anglosphere_primer.pdf

Berlin, Isaiah, 'Two Concepts of Liberty', republished in *Four Essays on Liberty* (1969)

Dickinson, G. Lowes, *An Essay on the Civilisations of India, China & Japan* (1913)

Eisenstadt, S. N., *Japanese Civilization* (1995)

Elvin, Mark, *The Pattern of the Chinese Past* (1973)

Fei Hsiao-Tung, *Peasant Life in* China (1939)

Geertz, Clifford, *Agricultural Involution* (1968)

Hajnal, John, 'European Marriage Patterns in Perspective' in D. V. Glass and D. E. C. Eversley (eds), *Population in History* (1965)

Hayami, Akira, 'A Great Transformation: Social and Economic Change in Sixteenth and Seventeenth Century Japan', *Bonner Zeitschrift fur Japanologie*, vol. 8, Bonn, 1986

Hershock, Peter, 'Chan Buddhism', *The Stanford Encyclopedia of Philosophy* (Spring 2017 Edition), Edward N. Zalta (cd.), URL = <https://plato.stanford.edu/archives/spr2017/entries/buddhism-chan/>

Hume, David, *Essays Literary, Moral and Political* (1873)

Huntington, Samuel P., *The Clash of Civilisations* (1996)

Jaspers, Karl, *The Origin and Goal of* History (1953)

Linton, Ralph, *The Study of Man* (1936)

Needham, Joseph, *Science and Civilization in China* (1954 onwards)
Pardue, Peter, 'Buddhism' in the *International Encyclopedia of the Social Sciences* (Macmillan, 1968)

Taine, Hippolyte, *Notes on England* (1873)

R. H. Tawney, R. H., *The Agrarian Problem of the Sixteenth Century*, (1912)

Tocqueville, Alexis de, *L'Ancien Regime* (1856)

Whitehead, Alfred North, *Religion in the Making* (1926)

Wright Mills, C. Wright, *The Sociological Imagination* (1956)

Hershock, Peter, 'Chan Buddhism', *The Stanford Encyclopedia of Philosophy* (Spring 2017 Edition), Edward N. Zalta (ed.), URL = <https://plato.stanford.edu/archives/spr2017/entries/buddhism-chan/>

The map used on pages 23, 60 and 117 are in the public domain, but from Blake, W., (pseud Thomas, H. Prescott), *The volume of the world: embracing the geography, history, and statistics, of the nations of the earth* ... (1855 edition), courtesy of Wikimedia Commons, provided by Geographicus Rare Antique Maps, a specialist dealer in rare maps and other cartography of the 15th, 16th, 17th, 18th and 19th centuries, as part of a cooperation project.

Thanks

These start with my three inspirational teachers at Sedbergh School – Andrew Morgan, David Alban and Bertie Mills. Then my excellent teachers at Oxford, James Campbell and Harry Pitt as undergraduates, and Keith Thomas as D. Phil supervisor. After that my anthropological advisors and inspirations: E. E. Evans-Pritchard, Christoph von Fürer-Haimendorf, Jack Goody and Ernest Gellner.

Friends and colleagues around the world: in China and the U.K. my various students, especially Wang Zilan, Li Shuo, Ma Xiao, Yan Xiao Xiao. In China, especially Professors Shengchun Zhou and Li Bozhong and my friends Duan Weihong and Yanfu Zu. In Japan, in particular Kenichi and Toshiko Nakamura, Osamu Saito, Kaoru Sugihara, Akira Hayami and Airi Tamura. In relation to Europe, particularly Peter Burke.

My friend and co-author Jamie Bruce Lockhart read the book several times and offered some useful suggestions on how to improve and shorten it.

Jaimie Norman helped design the book and cover.

My friends, co-workers and family: Iris Macfarlane, Mark Turin, the late Gerry Martin and always, and above all, Sarah Harrison.

The book is dedicated to the late, and sorely missed, John Davey, long-term friend, agent, publisher and advisor, who first suggested I wrote a book on China and then encouraged me in various stages of the writing of this wider book.

Printed in Great Britain
by Amazon